Necessary Words *for* Writers

What Do Those Agents and Editors Mean?

Donna Lee Anderson

abbott press®

A DIVISION OF WRITER'S DIGEST

Necessary Words for Writers
What Do Those Agents and Editors Mean?

Abbott Press books may be ordered through booksellers or by contacting:

Abbott Press
1663 Liberty Drive
Bloomington, IN 47403
www.abbottpress.com
Phone: 1-866-697-5310

ISBN: 978-1-4582-0642-8 (sc)
ISBN: 978-1-4582-0643-5 (e)

Library of Congress Control Number: 2012920021

Printed in the United States of America

Abbott Press rev. date: 11/01/2012

INTRODUCTION

When writers get together, they talk about writing. That's what this book is meant to be, a one-on-one, writer-to-writer conversation about the words and vocabulary used in the publishing industry.

This book got started during my first writer's conference. I met with an editor from a large publishing house and he said, "Just send me platform information, and a bio of course, and I'll need clips and sample chaps, and a synopsis . . . oh, just send a whole proposal package."

I didn't really understand most of the things he wanted but I didn't want to seem more stupid than I felt, so I wrote down the key words and looked them up. This is where my list started and continued. Every time I heard a new-to-me-word related to writing or the publishing business, it went on my list. (And as I'm working on this piece, I asked my writing partner if he knew what *scare quotes* were. He did and this is the answer: "Scare quotes are quotation marks around a term or word to indicate skepticism or derision and the word's normal meaning doesn't apply in this particular usage." Now I know.)

All the information in this book was garnered in the same way. I'd hear a word and then find the meaning by asking someone I thought should know (then verify the meaning by looking on the Internet), or I'd see a word with its meaning in a writing magazine (like *Writer's Digest* or *Poets and Writers* or *The Writer*), and I'd add it to my list. I also used Ask.com, Wikipedia. com, Write4kids.com, and sometimes just Googled the word.

This book is not meant as a dictionary but more of an explanation of the necessary publishing jargon a writer needs to know when dealing with the editors and agents in this business of publishing.

Of course there are words that aren't included here that are important, but I've left plenty of room for you to make your own notes and additions.

Donna Lee Anderson

ACQUISITION EDITOR

(See also Slush Pile)

The person at the publishing company who is in charge of receiving and rating manuscripts for possible publication.

> To be
> or
> not to be
> published.

In most publishing houses and agent offices, and even at small presses and some self-publishing companies, someone (or possibly a department) is designated to screen/read incoming submissions and then help decide if the company wants to pursue publishing that particular manuscript.

When the decision to publish is made, the acquisition editor will usually be responsible for taking a given manuscript through its various stages of editing until it's sent to the printer.

Unsolicited manuscripts (those that have not been requested) go into what's called a *slush pile* when they are received. Acquisition editors can and do pull manuscripts from this pile to read and decide what actions need to be taken. Does it get a form letter of rejection, or is it something the company is interested in pursuing?

This acquisition editor can also be charged with contacting certain authors and inviting them to write a new, particular kind of manuscript.

ACTION FICTION

Full and very detailed descriptions of physical actions that help the movement of a story line.

Romance, mystery, and adventure writers
all
incorporate these kinds of descriptions.

If action descriptions are meant to be the main thrust of the story, then it is probably action fiction. If your story describes in great detail (punch for punch) the danger of men fighting on top of a train in the Swiss Alps, it definitely is action fiction.

Descriptions of cowboy fights, war time battles, or vampire attacks can all be called action fiction; however, depending on how in-depth the details are written it could be classified as **General** or **Gritty** or **Edgy Action.**

<u>**General Action:**</u> Details about such things as a car race in progress, being on an African adventure, or about a couple on an Alpine ski trip could be for all ages to enjoy and is called *general action.*

<u>**Edgy Action Fiction:**</u> Details written about a car crash and the bleeding afterward—but doesn't describe the smashing of the drivers head on the windshield is *edgy action.* The description of the animal attack (but only the aftermath confusion), or details about the ski trip that may show all the action (up to but not including sex) would be *edgy action,* action on the edge of having the details written in a too-graphic or too-realistic way.

<u>Gritty Action Fiction:</u> These actions would include *very graphic* descriptions that include explicit details of such things as bloody bones sticking out of a leg following the car crash, African adventures with vivid animal attacks including how it felt to have your face ripped off, or a ski trips that end with sex scenes. Showing explicit details about everything, and written with a specific audience in mind, showing every nasty or ugly detail is *gritty fiction*.

ADVANCE
(See also Royalties)

Money paid to the author before the book is actually ready to be sold to the public.

Up-front money
paid before the royalties start to roll in.

Author advances vary from publisher to publisher and may be negotiable when an author signs the contract to sell their book. If an author has an agent, then the agent will usually negotiate for the author.

The *advance* is just that—an advance against future earnings—until the book sales generate enough money to pay back the advance to the publisher, and then the author will get paid again (and those proceeds are called *royalties*).

ADVANCE READER COPY (ARC)

Early copies of a book that the publisher sends to reviewers and interviewers.

A preview
of coming
attractions.

An Advanced Readers Copy (ARC) is sent to interviewers and reviewers so they can read the book (or at least part of it) in advance of author interviews or publicity appearances. These copies can also enable people to write reviews (yes, to advertise your book) in newspapers and magazines and to stimulate interest that could get the author interviews on TV, on the radio, or in print. Some interviewers will ask for a short synopsis or blurb about the book in lieu of a copy. And, sending an ARC to the author is considered a courtesy but not a *necessity* by some publishers.

Self-published writer's sometimes forget to include this expense in their budget and should be reminded that sending out copies of the book can help sales, and should be part of the marketing plan. Anything that the author can do to help the sales of the book is certainly beneficial to everyone, self-published or not.

AGENTS
(See also Representative)

People who can represent you and help with the business side of selling your writing to potential publishers.

*Who came first,
the agent or the publisher?*

Finding an agent to work with is sometimes a little tricky. Not all agents represent all kinds of writing (genres). Most specialize, so the writer will need to do some homework. Does a given agent represent fiction or non-fiction, or are they only interested in just a particular genre? A large agency full of many agents will probably include someone who works with your particular genre and writing style but it's up to you find and send to the correct agent.

Although having an agent to help you with your quest to be published is beneficial and remembering that some publishing houses do not accept un-agented material, some publishers do still allow un-solicited manuscripts to be submitted. Check the web site of an agent or publisher (in question) to see guidelines.

Some ways to find an agent:

Several magazines like *Poet's and Writer's* and *Writers Digest* and *The Writer, and* newsletters from the *SCBWI* and *Writers World* and *Writers Digest* keep current lists of agents for their subscribers, and they update these lists regularly. Some are free but if you're in the market for an agent, it may be worth a subscription price to be able to access the lists of these on-line newsletters.

Also look in directories of publications such as *Writer's Guide.* It is a large book available at bookstores, but they are also available at most public libraries.

Another place to look for a suitable match is to attend writer's conferences and make appointments with representatives from several offices. Bios for each agent will be furnished and you'll easily see which one is looking for a writer just like you. Many contracts and book deals have resulted from such appointments.

Things to know about agents:

They *do* move around to different agencies and sometimes open their own offices. To make sure the contact information is correct, try calling the agency and having a brief conversation with the receptionist. It could be very beneficial and enlightening. Make sure you have the *correct spelling* of the agent's name and their *correct title* and the *correct address*.

An agent belonging to the Association of Author's Representatives, Inc. (AAR), has committed to following certain guidelines and rules and can be expected to be creditable.

ANACHRONISM

A statement or situation that is not correct for this timeline.

Something that just could
<u>not</u> have been.

Anachronism means an action or spoken statement attributed to a specific time frame that just wouldn't be possible in this stories time and setting.

Example:
If you write about a knight in medieval days finishing a fight and using a GPS to find his way back to camp, or lighting a cigarette with a lighter as he rides back to camp on his motorcycle—those are anachronisms. Neither GPS's nor cigarettes nor motorcycles were available or used in this time period or in this world.

These are inaccurate details or anachronisms.

ANECDOTE

Usually a short account of an interesting or humorous event or situation.

> Did you hear
> the one about . . .

Although there are no rules on the length of an anecdote, they are usually very short. Now you say *how short is short*? They need to be as long as it takes to tell the story and get the point across.

Readers Digest is famous for its anecdotes—those short humorous paragraphs at the bottom of their pages. They are short because that publication requires that length, but other publications could have different criteria. Magazine, newspapers, newsletters, and other publications will have guidelines for this short, short story or anecdote submission, and that will dictate the length of the piece.

When telling a specific story or happening that has a humorous or strange climax, usually shorter is better. Writers get more *zing* in the prose that drops the ending on the reader, and then the story is finished. If you go on too long with the details, it could lose its punch or maybe even the point of the story.

ANTAGONIST
(See also Conflict)

Someone who offers resistance or opposition in your written piece.

Stir up the works

by

adding an antagonist

The antagonist is the main opponent of the protagonist (hero or heroine). They are a major character or group of characters, or even a happening that is distinctive and significant to the story, and they can further the story by adding a problem to be worked out. (They could be the part that gives a point to the story.)

Evoking feelings by introducing an opponent of the other character(s) or situation is just one way to add spice to a story. Introducing an antagonist will also add interest and perhaps depth.

Antagonist should not to be confused with a protagonist (who usually is the main character of a story); however the antagonist (the bad guy) can certainly be one of the main characters too.

ANTHOLOGY
(See also Story Collection)

A collection of stories or poems published in one book, and contains more than one author's writings.

Being published in an anthology
is a good way
to start your publishing life.

Organizations, such as women's clubs, churches, and writing groups, often gather to contribute to an anthology. It is usually a compilation of short stories or poems or essays written around a central theme. Individual contributions are from several writers, as opposed to just one author.

Sometimes a contest is held by a magazine or a publisher where the prize is having your contribution published in this anthology. It is not unusual for the rules or guidelines of an anthology contest to state that a committee will decide which ones are to be published. A small entry fee for the contest is not unusual, but *beware* if the contest rules ask for large sums of money or request you buy several books in order for your work to be included in the book (the anthology). Such tactics are often the mark of a scam.

Not only beginning writers appear in anthologies. Stephen King is one of the many seasoned authors that enjoy adding some of his short stories and thoughts to collections.

Anthologies are very popular for teaching purposes too. Having diverse styles of writing from several different writers, all in one book is a useful tool for seeing different uses of voice, point-of-view, and styles.

APPENDIX
(See also Index and Bibliography)

The printed matter at the back of a book.

More stuff the author wants
the reader to know.

Especially with nonfiction, notes regarding research or reference information are usually listed at the back of the book. This information is in an appendix. This section may be an index or a bibliography, the two main types of appendixes.

Information in this appendix may also include suggested additional reading on the book's topic and/or the credentials of the author (such as why he is knowledgeable about the topic).

ARC
(See also Advance Reader Copy)

Early copies of a book that the publisher sends to reviewers and interviewers.

A peek
at the
finished product.

An Advance Readers Copy (ARC) is sent to interviewers and reviewers so they can read the book in advance of author interviews, or publicity appearances. These copies also enable people to write reviews.

(See Advance Reader Copy for more information.)

ARTICLE

Magazines and newspapers use articles (usually non-fiction stories).

Another good way
to start
your publishing career.

Open any magazine and you'll see written pieces that are usually non-fiction. These are called articles. Non-fiction stories or how-to instructions in a magazine or newspaper can also be considered articles for readers to enjoy.

Fictional stories (even if based on factual information) probably wouldn't be considered articles. Instead, they would be called a piece, manuscript, or maybe just a story.

The length of an article depends on the request or guidelines set out by the publisher.

AUDIENCE
(See also Genre)

People who will want to read the book or about the subject you write. The reader you are writing for.

Others
(outside of your family)
who want to read your type of writing.

Because a writer has a story to tell, as soon as it's finished and ready for consumption, they look for someone to read their piece. Often the first step is to look for a publisher. During this process, one of the first questions the writer might be asked is: "In what genre should this story be included?" or "Who is the story aimed at?" or "Who is the audience for this piece?"

Most writers know in advance the answer to these questions. They are writing a specific type of story that will appeal to people who like to read in that genre.

Mystery writers could write with the YA (young adult) or adult audience in mind; romance writers could write towards a historical or modern romance audience; and children's books could be written with a certain age group in mind. All these potential readers are the audience. There are many cross-over audiences too. Harry Potter is only one case in point.

Knowing your audience before you write helps with dialogue and descriptions.

Note:
The words *reader* and *audience* are mostly interchangeable in the writing world

AUTHOR
(See also Writer)

Authors are anyone who writes, and especially published writers.

Author! Author!
Words you'd love to hear.

It's a very exciting time in a writer's life when their first piece is published, and it's also when a writer transitions and becomes an author.

Painters create masterpieces or maybe just something for the dining room wall. Sculptors create beautiful figurines and statues or perhaps something to give to their Mom. Writers create literary manuscripts or perhaps just stories for their Grandchild. No matter why you create, it is wonderful to be recognized. Becoming a published author is one form of recognition.

Not all writers aspire to being published and some decide to publish their own works. Validation for a writer comes in many forms. Accolades from your family and friends are nice, as is being published and having strangers enjoy your writing.

No matter why you write, if it pleases you to create, keep writing. Being published is not necessary for everyone.

AUTHOR BIOGRAPHY/BIO
(See also Bio, Resume, and Platform)

Information and facts about the author.

Tell the world who you are!

In the non-fiction writing world, an account of your education and experiences that are germane to the particular subject that you are writing about is called a biography or bio (as opposed to a resume).

Traditionally, resumes tell of education and work experience, however in a bio/biography you are telling the publisher or agent that you are the right one to write this manuscript or piece because of specific experiences or education or background. The experience you list is also called a platform and this information could also be put into your query letter.

Example (Non-fiction):

The following would be appropriate if you want to write for a gardening magazine or have written a gardening book.

Having received a master's degree in Horticulture from the University of Florida,

I've been working with these Oncidiums (orchids) for more than twenty years.

During this time I developed the first Deluxe Purple Beauty Butterfly Orchid,

This book is a step-by-step guide on how you-can-do-this-too—from dirt to lovely flowers.

Example (Fiction):

A bio is useful to publishers so they can see what you've published before. It also helps to show them you understand something about the publishing world.

AUTOGRAPH(ING)

An author signing their published work.

> More sweet words to a writer:
> "Will you autograph your book?"

Next time you're just sitting and doodling, practice your autograph skills. Will you use your initials or spell your first name out in full? Or, maybe you'll want to include your middle name too?

One warning: after you've signed your name twenty times in a row, will you wish you'd used a shorter version?

Also, try not to forget that people like their autographs personalized. You might want to just sign the book to the *first name of the fan—To Joe—then signing your name,* thereby shortening your writing time on each book.

Signing your books is fun but writer's cramp is not a myth.

Examples:
The various autographs of Theodore Pritchard Van Sutton (depending on his mood):
To Sally Richfield, Enjoy! TPVS
To John—T. P. Van Sutton
To Peter Enjoy!-Theodore P. Van Sutton

. . . or to a friend-
Joe, Hope you enjoy this book. Ted

BABY BOOKS
(See also Children's Books)

These books are generally picture books and less than fifty words in length.

> Babies' first introduction
> to a lifetime of pleasure.

These first books can be lullabies, nursery rhymes, finger play (*Itsy Bitsy Spider*), or wordless books with just pictures, or perhaps things to feel.

The length and format varies with the content, and the word count is usually under the 50 word range.

BACKLIST

A publisher's list of all in-house books that are being kept in print.

> You want your book
> Placed
> on this list.

After your book is published and distributed to the bookstores, perhaps it will become a big hit with the public, and perhaps it will be on the Best Seller list, and perhaps there will be another print run. If your book continues to sell at a good rate, perhaps there will be a third printing. If this popularity with the public keeps up, you will be *backlisted*. This is a publisher's term for a list of all the books that they keep in print because of the public demand.

A writer can only aspire to having a manuscript that, when published, can and will stand the test of time and reader scrutiny so that repeated printings are made and this title stays on the backlist of their publisher.

Even books like *Catcher on the Rye* by J.D. Salinger, which has sold upward of two hundred thousand copies a year, will be considered backlist—not new this year but still selling.

BACK MATTER
(See also Front Matter, Index, Bibliography, and Appendix)

All the stuff written and put at the end of a non-fiction book (such as the glossary or index) or in a fiction book (such as the author info, etc.).

After the main story . . .
the back pages.

With non-fiction books, the back matter could include a glossary of terms, an index, maps of interest to the topic of the book, recommendations of similar books, advertisements about other books this publisher has printed or that this author has published, or any other information the publisher wants the reader to know.

In fiction writing, the pages at the end of the book could tell you about the author, or may include a blurb about an upcoming book, or a recommendation to the reader (i.e. If you liked this book you might enjoy _Title of a Specific Book_ by _Name of Author_).

BACKSTORY
(See also Flashbacks, Prologue, and Introduction)

What happened to your characters, or the action before *this* story started.

A little info

To

Enhance the <u>now</u> story.

Sometimes a prologue or an introductory chapter is needed in a novel to impart some necessary information on what previously has been happening before the story actually starts. It may get the reader up-to-speed on a particular character and his flaws, or the world events at the time of this story, or any other necessary imparting of details to help the reader's understanding, and bring him right into the story.

A *backstory* can also be woven into the plot by using flashbacks or conversation between characters, or memories related through dreams. If backstory information is needed, putting it into the story is usually preferable, rather than just a statement at the beginning of the piece.

BAR CODE
(See also ISBN)

A system of lines, bars, and numbers printed on a book cover that gives information about the book.

Now
they can find it!

This system of lines, bars, and numbers is used around the world in the book industry to help book distributors and booksellers with inventory and ordering. When the code is read by a scanner, it reveals the language the book was printed in, the original price of the book, and the ISBN (International Standard Book Number).

Note:
Bar codes are used on many, many other products for identification purposes too.

BEACH BOOK
(See also Chick Lit, Lad Lit, Mom Lit, Gay Lit, and Gray Lit)

Quick reads that are perfect for vacations and reading while sitting on the beach.

Happy and/or romantic novels
or
maybe just a book of short stories.

Chic Lit or any of the 'Lit' books (Mom Lit, Cougar Lit, Dad Lit, Gray Lit, etc.) could be called Beach Books or Vacation Books. They are usually shorter in length and quick reads, made up of short chapters, simple plots, and with a happy ending.

These same books are good for train or airplane rides or cruises or commuters. Not heavy subjects and usually meant to entertain, not educate.

BIBLIOGRAPY

A list of papers, books, or sources for information that is referenced in a manuscript.

> Giving credit
> where credit is due.

In the back of a non-fiction book, you will usually find an index or appendix that includes identification of research or resource material used to write the book.

Note:
Although the author's platform could be part of a bibliography, (why he is an expert), this is not usual.

BIOGRAPHY/BIO
(See also Author Bio, Resume and Platform)

Information about your writing career—your credentials.

The resume of your writing skills.

Bio's are a necessary parts of a query or proposal.

By the time you're ready to submit your work to a publisher or agent, you will probably have already written resumes or filled out employment applications. Think of a biography or bio as a resume of your writing; as if you were applying to a publisher or agent for a job of writing. It shows what you know about the subject you are touting in your writing and what you have written before.

For non-fiction:

In your bio you will want to show especially the education and experience you have that's applicable to the subject you are writing about now, or experiences you've had in the field that is germane to the subject of the writing. The fact that you have a degree in Mechanical Engineering would be of little interest if you write a piece on raising tulips in a milk carton, but would be of interest to automotive magazine publishers. Relevant travels or people you have interviewed should be included as part of a bio too (where germane).

Note:

All writers should have at-the-ready a one-page bio, a one paragraph bio, an in-depth bio of five or more (as necessary) pages. Just remember—this is supposed to be about your writing and any employment or education or perhaps even travel that relates to it.

BLACK HUMOR
(See also Dark Fiction and Noir)

Making light of unhappiness or disasters or any other serious situation.

> Laughing at things
> that are normally not funny.

Black or dark or noir humor can be found prolifically in cartoons. When you see the wife hitting the husband on the head with a frying pan, or when you see a road-runner push a coyote off a cliff, it is meant to be humorous, but if the act actually happened it would certainly not be funny.

Dark or black or noir humor can also be utilized when the protagonist is being self-effacing or self-deprecating, or maybe it's directed at one of the supporting characters in your piece. During WWII the writers directed abuse and dark humor towards the Germans and Japanese. Also, some black magic and sorcery stories could be considered dark or black humor.

Noir is a kind of film that was made especially during the 1940s and 1950s. It depicted a negative, cynical view of life, often focusing on crime and vice in cities. These films used dark or black humor.

BLOG

Internet sites used for journaling or for airing your ongoing thoughts.

> Some Blogging sites
> have become a venting source,
> but you can find info there too.

To blog (short for Web log) is to keep a personal on-going conversation on the Internet, or it can be a collaborative space with several people adding their thoughts.

The blog subject can be whatever you want it to be, on any subject, and so far, there are no real rules. New input shows up at the top and all the old stuff stays on the site.

There can also be linking sites and email capability, however the site itself is usually not a chat room or email site.

BLUELINE COPY

The final copy before the manuscript goes to the printer.

Last stop
before it's a printed book.

After all the editing is finished and the cover is decided, then the manuscript is formatted and set to be published. This is a blueline copy. (Not to be confused with an editor that corrects a manuscript using a blue pencil.)

BLUE PENCIL COPY
(See also Edit and Blueline Copy)

Editorial marks and corrections made on a manuscript or movie script.

Fixing and changing
suggestions.

Editors may use a blue pencil or red pencil to note their suggested changes to a manuscript, or make suggestions verbally. You'll have to admit using a colored pencil makes it easier to see what they suggest.

BLURB
(See also Synopsis and Elevator Speech)

A short synopsis of your written piece

A
very, very
short synopsis.

"What's your story about?" is a question you will be asked as a writer. Much like the question "How are you?" the speaker doesn't want to hear all the details. They expect to hear a sentence or two telling them the gist of the story—a blurb.

A written blurb is usually found on the back cover of the book and is supposed to help the reader decide if they want to read the story inside. It should only hit on major points of the story, and it should only be a few sentences long.

Example:
During the middle-ages, Jonathan Michelehouse is home from the wars and finds his beloved wife is now a maid in the house of his evil brother—the bother that killed their father. To make matters even worse, they are living in the castle FIFTH HOUSE, which belongs to Jonathan because he is the eldest son.

BODY OF WORK
(See also Drek)

A manuscript—the piece itself is the body of the work.

Either a work in progress

or

work that's finished.

While you are working on your story (either short story or longer manuscript in fiction, non-fiction, or poetry), the manuscript itself is referred to as your body of work.

This could also refer to a complete collection of an author's manuscripts.

BOOK

Pages of a manuscript, published, bound and with covers.

> Hardcover or softcover,
> it's still a book.

The definition *book* is pretty straightforward. A written or printed body of work consisting of pages sewn or glued together (along one side), and bound in covers that is not a periodical or magazine.

BOOK DISTRIBUTOR

Companies that deliver the published books to booksellers.

Gotta
get it out there.

After a book is published (printed in book form), it needs to be taken to places where the reader can purchase it. Companies that move these books are called distributors.

If you self-publish it is good to be associated with a local distributor and even a national company. If you are in doubt as to whom to call, ask your local bookstore for names of their distributors.

BOOK DOCTOR

Book doctors help fix problems in a book. They could also be called editors.

Finding and fixing
is their job.

Editing and proof reading are necessary tools for a writer. Usually a writer can find the misspelled words and lack of punctuation, but when it comes to one's own work, POV (point of view), and changes in voice are harder to put a finger on (in your own work.)

After a book if finished sometimes a book doctor is a good way to give a final polish to your work. They can call to the writer's attention such things as a weak opening or overuse of a certain words, or story points that need bolstering.

BOOK LIST

A publisher's list of titles it has published in a particular genre.

Publishers print their books in cycles; some print twice a year and some just once. The catalog of their most recent books published is called a book list.

Don't confuse BOOK LIST with the BACK LIST which is a list of books still being printed no matter how long ago it was published for the first time.

Hint: A tool for finding a publisher: You can call their office and ask for a book list or catalog. They will send you a copy, e-mail it to you, or tell you where to find it on the Internet, and then you can see which genres it prints, and how your work might fit.

BOOK PACKAGER

A company that works with writers, editors, illustrators, etc. to put a book together to sell to a publisher.

> The gatherer
> of all the pertinent parts,
> so a book can be published.

Self publishing and working with a Book Packager is not necessarily the same.

With a Packager, a writer turns over their manuscript to a company that will edit it, see to the layout and see to the placing of any illustrations that might be needed. When the book is ready to be printed, it is then sold to a publisher.

In self publishing, the writer could possibly do all this work on their own.

BOOK PROPOSAL
(See also Proposal)

Documents that will show and convince a publisher to buy your piece.

First comes the cover/query letter
and then . . .

Usually book proposals are needed for non-fiction books. This book proposal is much like a marriage proposal in that you ask another to be your partner for the life of the book.

Non-fiction Book Proposals do not vary much in the list of things you will need to send:

Cover letter: Tell them who you are, what you wrote, why you are qualified to write it.

Table of Contents: Not of the book, but of the package/proposal you are sending.

Bio: About the Author (and including a picture is good).

Marketing Plan: Possible places you could sell your book or make appearances, information about your audience, or generally what you think you can do to help sell your book.

Competition: Who is writing similar books?

Synopsis: Look at guidelines for length of expected synopsis. Some publishes require a one page, some require multiple pages, and some want only a paragraph.

Summary of manuscript (each publisher and agent has its own guidelines for a synopsis)**: Example:** By *chapter*: (i.e. Chapter 1-Harry meets Sally. Chapter 2-Harry and Sally have a fight about driving. Chapter 3-etc.), or by *major story points*: After a fight, Harry kills Sally and spends the next several days trying to dispose of the body, escapes a police raid, etc.

Sample Chapters: These should be the first two to five chapters from you book (or whole book in the case of a children's book). Usually the guidelines will dictate how much the agent/publisher wants to see.

Note:

There are many good books to teach you about writing and presenting a proposal. Two recommendations are:

For Non-fiction:
How to Write a Non-fiction Book Proposal
by Stephan Blake Mettee (Quill-Driver)

For Fiction:
Write the Perfect Book Proposal: 10 that sold and why.
by Jeff Herman and Deborah Levine Herman (John Wiley & Sons, Inc.)

BOOK RETURNS

Bookstores return unsold books to the publisher.

Don't confuse this
with library returns.

When a new book is published, booksellers and distributors order the amount of books they expect to sell. If they don't sell them in a certain time-frame, they are allowed to return the excess books to the publisher.

BOOKSELLERS

Bookstores, airports, grocery stores, and anywhere else that sells books.

Publishers
and self-published authors alike
use bookseller conferences to network.

The definition of a bookseller is a place that sells books, such as bookstores. Writer's of self published works also fall under this definition.

Booksellers have conferences and meetings in order to preview upcoming publications. At a bookseller's conference, publishers and self-published authors come from all over the map to see what is being showcased and to sell what they hope will be the next best seller. Usually there are booths set up, and sometimes the public is invited. Almost every region has its own conference. Some of the bigger and better known are in Los Angeles, New York and Chicago.

You may also find book distributors at these bookseller conferences.

BOOKS IN PRINT

A list of books in print or about to be printed based on the ISBN numbers given to them by them by publishers.

So many books,
so little time to read them all.

This very large database is managed by R. R. Bowker. They list books in print or about to be printed based on the ISBN numbers issued to them.

BREVITY

Writing a piece succinctly and making it short (especially in magazines and newspapers).

How long is short?
Guidelines rule.

More is not always *better* in writing. The guidelines of a publication will tell you how many words are expected in a piece and brevity is usually the name of the game.

Some writers take a subject and start writing, then pare it down to the length or word count that's asked for. Deleting all unnecessary adverbs (look for *ly* words), and noting which *adjectives* are needed and eliminating those that are just floating around can make a tighter and stronger statement.

Children's stories (fiction and non-fiction) are a good example of brevity. Each age group has a guideline dictating a certain amount of words). Pre-readers or picture books may have as few as ten sentences spread out over many pages, while a chap book for the Tween readers can be as long as one-hundred-fifty pages. (See Children's Books for more details.)

BUSINESS CARDS

A small card that states your name, e-mail address, telephone number, and perhaps your mailing address—and don't forget your website.

Tell the world
you're a professional.

Business cards are used in the writing world (as in other businesses) to help advertise the fact that a person is serious about this business of writing, and that they understand how to introduce themselves in a business-like manner. These cards can be printed professionally or on your own computer. They also can be an advertisement of your up-coming book (imprinted with a picture of the cover).

Some try for the cutesy look with kittens or airplanes on their business cards, while some try to crowd so much information on the card that it stops being a business card and becomes a miniature bio. Your business card should show your name, title, (like Author or Columnist or Artist), and contact information. A professional printer will have samples for you to choose from and the cost is very nominal.

You may hear book advertising advice that says to put a copy of your published book cover on your business cards. If you use them only at book signings or readings, this is a fun advertising gimmick, but beware!!! This is not a business card that says professional business person.

And don't forget, with any kind of luck, this won't be the *only* book you will publish, so you might want both kinds of cards—one for advertising and one for business purposes.

BYLINE

When your name is printed at the top (or bottom) of your article or piece in a newspaper or magazine, you have a byline.

Identification
of the writer.

When you have a magazine article or newspaper column published, and your name is printed at the top by the title or at the bottom of the piece, that's called a byline. And if they include a picture too, it's even better.

CAREER BOOKS
(And magazines)

Any book(s) that will give you information about a career or help you further your chosen profession (especially in writing).

And don't forget those
writers' magazines
that educate and give advice.

Career books are the ultimate how-to books. They give you information and instructions about many things you might need on your road to success. You can find on-the-job descriptions, information about dress codes, and perhaps what studies are required to prepare for a given career.

For writers, the how-to career books can offer instruction about sentence structure, point of view (POV), character development, plotting, and everything else that makes a story readable and ultimately saleable. You could also find writer conference information, particulars on your specific genre, or guidelines and submission rules for submitting to publishers and agents. Some articles even spell out specifics, like how to write queries and proposals.

In magazines such as *The Writer* or *Writer's Digest* or *Poets and Writers*, articles are written in every issue to explain and help with a wide range of writers problems such as plotting or character development. Sometimes they include interviews with authors where they share their writing secrets.

For every writing question, there are several books and magazines to tell you everything you might want to know.

CHAP BOOKS

Children's Books written with chapters, or a chap book of poetry.

> One more step up in reading growth of a child,
> or do you mean a book of poetry?

When children graduate from the sitting-on-your-lap-reading phase to reading to themselves, we stay in attendance to help with those pesky new words. After this stage comes the books with the story divided up into chapters (chap books), just like grown-ups read.

Stories are age appropriate and vary in length and subject matter. Most children find this a proud, big step in their reading abilities.

Adult fiction books are mostly chapter books but this phrase refers especially to children's books.

The definition of a poetry chapbook is a little different. The word comes from the Old English word *céap*, meaning cheap. They were inexpensive books of folded paper (one large sheet being folded to produce twenty-four pages) and were often shoddily made. Today, they are still only about twenty-four to fifty pages, but they are every bit as high quality poetry as larger (and more expensive) books.

CHARACTER DEVELOPMENT

Showing the people in your story as having emotions and feelings and also showing them as they change. The writer also exposes details of the characters' lives so the reader knows them well.

Making the story characters real.

In order to develop a character in a story, you don't necessarily have to list the color of their eyes or say how tall they are. Instead, you can show the reader what they are like by how they react in a situation, by their dialogue, or by revealing some important details about their lives, background or personality.

Readers will have their own mental picture of your character, especially if you (the writer) can show their feelings and quirks, take a character from start to finish of a situation, and then show the aftermath/consequences of their actions. It will help give the character the depth and development needed to further the plot and, hopefully keep your reader emotionally invested.

CHARACTERS

All the actors (people or not) in your story.

> Some characters aren't people,
> Especially in children's books.

Not all stories have people in them but if it does, these people are called characters. And yes, if you have inanimate things taking on human characteristics like talking plants or even rocks . . . they are called characters too.

Characters help to tell the story and do the actions that make the plot move on to the conclusion. A writer can have characters explain problems, be the problem, talk about the problem, help find the solutions, and make closing statements. They are totally involved in the story.

CHIC LIT/CHICK FICTION

Books with stories about strong women and how they handle life's issues in their pursuit of a perfect partner.

Do you think more chick lit books
are read in the bathtub
than in the library?

More and more women enjoy these books that are different from standard romance novels. They can have shorter chapters, fewer characters and although they are both well written, these chic-lit books do not deal with earth shaking problems. The subject matter is usually about the young professional woman, and her adventures in finding that special someone to share her life.

The protagonist (main character) is usually a strong working woman that solves what ever problem is presented in her daily life and usually leaves the reader happy with the outcome.

Now, here's a secret. More and more men are enjoying these stories too and there is a parallel writing genre for guys called Lad Lit.

Well written stories that make you happy when you read them—what could be better for men or women?

CHILDREN'S BOOKS

Young adult, preteen/tween, early reader, young reader, picture, pre-reader, and chap books are all considered books for children.

Explore your inner child;
write for children.

There are several distinct types of reading material for children:

Baby books or **pre-reader books** or **picture books** are all for a reader and a non-reader to experience together (usually for a child under the age of three). Some of these pre-reader books have little or no words, just pictures or textures for the child to feel. These could also be a picture book that (after several readings) a young child could *pretend to read* to themselves (Usually not more than 50 words). Pure picture books are balanced between text and pictures—each adding to the story.

Early Reader books usually have few pages, large print and a very short story consisting of short sentences and not too long (usually around 32 pages).

A **Young Reader** will have graduated to **Chap Books** (books that contain short chapters but a simpler story line than Tween Books).

Tween or a **Pre-teen** book is for the ten to thirteen year old (approximately). These readers are not quite a teen but too old for the young reader books. The Twilight Series could be considered a **Tween Book**.

Young Adult books are written with an adult level vocabulary, but keeping in mind the subjects that interest this age group of fourteen and upward (snow boarding, skate boarding, dating, parent/child relationships, etc.)

Remember it is difficult to put a *reading group age* on any children's books except for the pre-reader or picture book. Reading skills and interests are accomplished at a different rate of speed for every child, however some books such as *Harry Potter* or *Little House on the Prairie* are a couple of books that appeals to every age group after the pre-reader age (and even adults).

CINE LIT

Books written *after* the movie script is written, or a book written expressly for movie adaptation purposes.

Which came first,
the movie or the book?

(This phrase was explained at a writer's conference in Oregon at a screen writing workshop.)

One Cine Lit that started as a television show and then made into a book was the *Murder She Wrote* television series. It was a very popular show and the demand for books soon produced a whole series. Currently, the television show Castle started first and now books are showing up on book selves. Many viewers assumed these books came first, but they didn't.

An example of books written expressly for adaptation to a movie are the numerous. Walt Disney's *Shreck* is one that was written with making a movie in mind.

If this is the kind of writing you are interested in, living and being close to the cinema making center would definitely be a plus.

CLIPS

Copies of what you have written and published.

Show-and-tell
of your
Publishing history.

Copies of any articles or short stories you have published are called clips.

All genres of writing are usable as clips. If you write articles for the *Day-Care Newsletter* and it is distributed, then you've been published. If you write your company bulletin or if you write in-house company manuals, that is all considered published material and copies of these are called clips.

When sending a query letter or book proposal, clips are a good thing to include so that the publisher or agent will know you *can* write, *how* you write, and that you know about deadlines and guidelines. How many clips should be included? Usually not more than three clips of articles, and not more than two stories. However, you can include a list of what you published so the publisher or agent can see what types of experiences you've had.

COFFEE TABLE BOOKS

Those large books of photographs that are left out for all to enjoy (especially visitors).

Picture books
for grown-ups.

Although some homes don't actually have coffee-tables (that small table in front of the couch), these coffee-table books full of beautiful pictures of exotic places and things, are favored by many decorators. They are usually a theme book (all on one subject) and are over-sized to show the subject matter to its best advantage.

COLUMNIST/COLUMN

Newspapers and magazines contain written pieces that are sometimes called columns, which are written by columnists.

By-lines
are the best.

In a newspaper, if the story isn't about news, then it could be considered a column. In a magazine most stories are considered columns.

Writers who are columnist are happy when their work is published in a newspaper or magazine on an on-going schedule. Sometimes the writer will get paid for each column or article, or perhaps will be on a salary from the publication, and having their name published at the beginning (or the end) of their piece is not only good for the writer's bio, but is a definite plus when establishing a platform.

COMMENTS

Notes to the writer from a publisher or agent (or readers).

Direction
or
advice
regarding a piece.

After you submit your query or proposal, you may get a message from the publisher or agent. They will sometimes send a few comments regarding your submitted piece (or maybe even on form rejection letters). Use these comments, positive or negative, to help you become a better writer.

Samples comments:
This manuscript is in need of a professional editing.
It is of course up to you if you hire a professional editor to help you before you send it out again, but it is a comment to take seriously. It might refer to POV or any number of things that were noticed, but a professional editor can look at a sample and help you decide if you want to have the full manuscript edited or not before you send it out again.

This piece is not something we would publish.
This probably means you didn't do your homework before you sent it out and this publisher/agent does not "do" or "represent" this genre.

Please rewrite the opening chapter(s) to make a stronger hook for the reader and resubmit.
These lovely words would be an invitation to rewrite the first chapter(s) and re-submit to this person/publisher. It says there is interest and possibly a contract in sight.

And don't forget those *comments from your readers*. Very valuable info and feedback to have.

COMMERCIAL FICTION

Any books that sell well—romance, detective, sci-fi, how-to, etc.

Popular reads,
available everywhere.

It's easy to see what commercial fiction is—just look in any supermarket or bookstore at the racks holding "Just Arrived" or "Best Seller" books. Hardback and paperbacks alike fall into this category.

Romance and mystery stories are popular genres, but more and more biographies, autobiographies, and self-help books are becoming popular too. No, they're not all fiction, but they certainly are commercial.

Generally books are divided into literary and commercial fiction. The biggest difference between the two is that editors expect to make a bigger profit from commercial books but it's not always true about literary works.

COMPARISONS

Comparing your piece or your style to another writer or book.

Just who
do you write like?

A way to tell an agent or publisher what your writing is like, is to make a comparison to another writer. You might say, "I write in the same fashion as Stephen King, only no one dies."

Or you could say, "My books would be on the self in the library next to Michael Creighton."

This is giving a comparison to your work, a handy way to show the agent or publisher that you know your audience.

COMPUTER SOFTWARE AND PROGRAMS

How-to software with explicit instructions for writers.

You can find
interesting how-to-write stuff
on-line too.

Many computer software programs have been developed to help writers. You can get plotting help, outlining lessons, and story ideas and help for that writer's block.

You also can find Internet sites that can help you find seminars and conferences in your area, and sites that offer practice writing. Some sites charge but many are free. It never hurts to practice, and it does start the juices flowing again if you're having a slowdown of ideas.

To find a particular software program, look in writer's magazines such as *Writer's Digest* or *Poets and Writers*, or at bookstores and computer stores. Installation is usually easy with explicit directions included in the package.

CONCEPT

An abstract idea that may be the beginning of an article, story, or book.

> The birth
> of a story idea.

Especially in non-fiction, editors will ask for the idea or concept of the proposed piece.

Let's say your idea is to write a story about flowers that grow from a bulb. Your plan is to follow the growth from planting the bulb through the opening of the flower. This is the concept of what the story will be about.

CONFERENCE

Meetings with and/or conferring with an expert in a certain field, or with a publisher, agent, or lawyer—all are conferences.

Meetings meant to further
your writing career.

In non-fiction, attending a conference in the field you want to write about can be helpful. You can get inside opinions/information/heads-up to new things, or just network with people in the know.

A writer's conference could afford the writer meetings with editors from a publishing house or with a literary agent and can help a writer evaluate if their writing is ready for submission.

The information these people impart at the seminars could also tell a writer if they are pitching their manuscript in the correct genre and to the correct person that handles this genre. (For example: a mystery would not necessarily mean the piece is just for adults. It might fit into the young adult slot, or into the romance mystery genre.) Another plus is that it can help the writer determine if they are ready to be published or if more tweaking/editing is needed.

Also, when you receive a contract from a publisher, another conference you might need is with a lawyer so that you understand the legal terms regarding the upcoming publication of your work.

CONFLICT

The part of the plot showing what problem is to be solved in the story. Sometimes more than just a single conflict situation will add spice to a story.

> Indecision can be a conflict
> as much as a fight.

All stories have a conflict in them even if it is as minor as how to jump over the candlestick.

Conflict can be tension between characters or tension in the mind of just one person, but no matter how large or small, conflict can make the plot fuller and more interesting.

Note: The three parts of a story are hook, conflict and resolution.

CONTACT INFO
(See also Business Cards)

A writer's name, address, phone number, e-mail address, and don't forget to add website info (if you have one).

This is me!

Everywhere you turn in the writing world, you will be asked for contact information. The old fashioned way is to tell people your phone number or email address and stand by while they find a pencil and paper to write it down, or you can hand them a business card that contains everything they want to know.

When you send query letters or book proposals, contact information should include home address, home phone number, work phone number, email address (and your web site address, if you have one). Some writer's have a post office box for writing purposes so the daily home mail doesn't get mixed in; however, home addresses are indeed acceptable and used by the majority of writers until they get a writing office address.

CONTACTS
(See also Networking)

Anyone you meet who will help you in your writing career.

> Making contacts
> and
> networking
> is the name of the game.

    Meeting people that can help you in your publishing quest is important. This is no time to be shy. Writer's Conferences are a good place to meet these contacts and to network with publishers, agents, editors, and other writers. They are all good to know, even if you don't need their specific services or knowledge right now.

    Authors are usually very happy to talk about writing with other writers, and you never know when you will meet and get help from someone regarding a publisher for your piece or about someone that could represent your work.

CONTEST

Contests are one way publishers can meet new writers. A fee for entering is not unusual.

Beginning writers
can get practice
submitting and following the rules and guidelines.

It is valuable to know about contests. If you're entering one, you need to be sure it is a creditable publication or magazine or publishing entity offering a prize. A fee for entering is a way for the sponsoring company to control the type of entries. One theory is that if you have to pay money, you will abide by the rules.

Entering a contest is one way for a beginning writer to see how they stack up against other writers, and, maybe a way to get published faster. In some contests the prize is being printed in an anthology or magazine, however, beware of contests that require large entry fees or that offer to *let* you buy copies of a published book for large sums. These may not be legitimate contests.

Note about the rules and guidelines: When entering any competition, be sure to send *exactly* what is asked for in the submission rules or guidelines. Check the length and word count, check you margins, check the headings they request (where you name should and should not appear), write about the requested subject matter, and don't forget to include a SASE (self-addressed stamped envelope) if you submit by mail rather than on-line. This is so you can get comments on your writing or to hear back if you're a winner.

CONTRACT

A formal legal document that spells out what will happen to your manuscript, and perhaps any further manuscripts that follow, and the details regarding remuneration for the author.

Signing a contract
is a part of the writing world
you're probably looking forward to.

Contracts between a writer and an agent or publisher need to be treated very seriously.

Contracts differ in the writing world just as they do in any other profession or legal transaction. Before signing, don't forget that all contracts should be reviewed by a lawyer who is knowledgeable about the literary ins-and-outs. There will be things they will know to look for that you might not (For example: Is this contract for one book only or for all other books you write? or Who owns the rights after publication and for how long? or How will the writer be paid? These are just some of the things you need to know before you sign.)

Also look in the contract to find out about the advance and payment schedule, what part of the marketing the publisher will do, and when the publication date will be. There are many pieces to a contract, and they all should be thoroughly understood by the writer.

CONTRIBUTOR'S COPY

Anthologies and magazines often give the contributing authors copies of the published work as payment.

Reading your contributor's copy
is a good cure for the writing blahs.

Being a contributor to a publication means you have a piece (an article or story or poem that you wrote) in that publication. Compensation for writing this piece may be free copy or copies of the publication.

Writer's should be happy to have this copy of a book or publication with their work included because it makes for good clips, and might be a deal maker when you have a one-on-one meeting with an agent or editor, and you are able to show the magazine or anthology with your piece in it. Nothing says success better (for show-and-tell) when you meet one-on-one with an agent or publisher.

CO-PUBLISHING

More than one publisher working to get a book printed.

> Co-publishing isn't for everyone,
> but it works for some.

Self-publishing an anthology is a good way to explain co-publishing.

When several writers contribute to a book (either short stories or poems or a combination of both), and they share in the publishing duties. Probably there will be committees formed to see to the details; some would edit, some would see to getting the pages formatted, or some will see that the graphics are in camera-ready form. If all of the writers are working together and helping with the publishing duties, this is co-publishing.

Another kind of co-publishing is if two publishers work together to publish a book. This is *not* a common occurrence, but one example is if your fiction piece is medically technical in nature, it may happen that a fiction publisher *and* a scientific publisher would work together to get the book published and out to the public.

COPY EDITOR

Editors who prepare the last copy of the written pages for the printer.

The last look-through
before the book is printed.

After you have sold your manuscript to a publisher you will be dealing with several people under the title of editor.

One of the most important is the copy editor. They are the last one to look at and check the pages of your book before it goes to the printer. Spelling, layout, graphics, and/or picture placements are just a few things that are checked.

COPYRIGHT
(See also Rights)

The part of the contract that spells out who owns this piece of writing.

> Knowing who owns your work
> is important.

As soon as you write a piece you own the copyright. However, if you wish to publish it, then a contract will spell out who will have the rights of ownership of the piece you have written, and say who can publish this piece, and how long before the right-to-publish returns to you, the writer.

When you sign a contract you are assigning the rights to someone else, and that is a legal action. Before you sign a contract it might be sensible to have an attorney familiar with the writing world go over the contract with you so you understand *exactly* what you are signing away.

There are many rights besides the copyright to this piece that can be sold or given by the author. Here are some of the most common:

All Rights: Everything listed here and anything else a publisher might think up.

Electronic Rights: Printing or displaying your piece as it refers to computer technology (i.e. print on demand, e-books, CD's, etc.).

First Time Rights: This is the first time this piece has been printed and the publisher has the right to publish it only this first time.

Foreign Rights: Your piece printed anywhere except the United States. (Similar rules apply for English speaking rights.)

Hardcover or Trade/Paperback Rights: Permission to print your piece in a particular format.

North American Rights: A limit on the publisher to only publish this work for sale in North America (sometimes combined with English speaking rights).

One Time Rights: Publisher can print your piece only one time.

Paperback Rights: Your piece made into a softcover paperback as opposed to a hardcover format.

Second Serial Rights: Publisher can reprint after the piece is published the first time.

Secondary Rights: Publisher can reproduce the piece in other ways, such as audio books, movie or television script, or in condensed form in a magazine, etc.

Simultaneous Rights: Your piece can be published at the same time as others are publishing it.

Subsidiary Rights: Secondary rights and subsidiary rights go hand in hand. After the original publishing, your piece could be merchandised (figurines of your main characters, T-shirts, lunch boxes, etc.).

COUGAR LIT

Stories about older women looking for younger men for romantic interaction.

Romance
outside the box?

Under the genre of romance there are many sub-genres and cougar lit is one, along with chick lit, gay lit, gray lit, lad lit, mom lit, and many more.

In these cougar lit stories there will be an older, wealthy, educated woman approaching and contacting younger men who probably haven't had time to get wealthy yet, and probably will be of lesser income and possibly a blue collar type.

She will be the hunter, the younger man the prey.

COVER LETTER
(See also Query and Proposal)

A business letter sent to the publisher or agent that contains a few pieces of explicit information about the writer and their writing

Your first
sales pitch.

Wikipedia says: The rule of three is a writing principle that suggests that things that come in threes are inherently funnier, more satisfying, or more effective than other numbers of things. The reader or audience of this form of text is also more likely to remember information if it is written in groups of threes.

Good cover letters for queries or book proposals follow the rule of three:

. . . Include the name of your submission at least **3** times in the cover letter,

. . . The letter should contain no more than **3** paragraphs for a story or poem submission, no more than **3** pages for a longer novel,

. . . And there are **3** important things to mention in this letter:

. . . What genre you feel this fits into,

. . . For non-fiction, why you are the best one to write this piece (give germane bio info and your platform),

. . . Provide comparisons to like works,

And . . . Don't forget to include a marketing plan—what you can do to help sell your book.

Cover letters for a submission to a magazine or newspaper probably won't be more than one (1) page, but these same rules (except for the marketing plan) can apply.

A cover letter should be written on good paper stock and be professionally formatted.

Look for sample letters at such places as Writer's Digest Magazine (it's on-line too), or in books specifically about writing query letters and proposals.

(Warning: Don't confuse this with a cover page which might only include the title of your book and author's name, or any other info like word count that the guidelines dictate.)

COVER PAGE
(See also Cover Letter)

A page presented on top of the submission showing the name of the piece, the author's name, and the word count (or page count if requested).

Used especially
when submitting a novel manuscript.

When you are sending a hard copy of your manuscript to a publisher or agent, the cover page should be the first thing that is seen when a submission box is opened in their office. It should contain the name of the manuscript and the author's name. This information is centered on the page and the name of the manuscript can be in all CAPS but it's not necessary.

Some submission guidelines ask for page count or word count to be included on the cover page, but should not be included unless it's asked for.

Don't confuse a *cover page* with a *cover letter*, which will include not only words count of your manuscript, but bio info, and a short synopsis.

Sometimes sending a cover page on top of all the information (your cover letter/manuscript/bio) is a helpful tool for the receiving office so that it gets routed to the person that requested it. Anything that can help get it into the right hands quickly is a good thing.

COZY MYSTERY

This is a mystery that is solved by an everyday person rather than the police or law enforcement.

Homey stories
with whodunit action.

The Cozy Mystery is a sub-genre of the bigger mystery group. As opposed to the police, these amateur detectives can be anyone. Perhaps the character is located in a small town where they know everyone, and with the help of gossip or maybe some facts overheard at the local diner; this person is able to solve the case. It's not unusual for this person to have an "in" at the police department—or maybe married to a police person or they are friends of someone at the precinct.

This sub-genre is basically a mystery in a cozy place solved by someone like Jessica Fletcher (*Murder She Wrote*) or Miss Marple.

The early cozy's usually had a woman (or two) as the detective(s), but this has enlarged to include men and even animals (cats and dogs and even monkeys have solved mysteries).

CRASH WRITING

Writing a complete story in a very short time frame.

Maybe your writing group
does this for fun.

Crash writing especially applies to poetry but prose can benefit from this too. It is usually a group that has gathered to write or entertain each other with their writing. They decide on a time frame and state a subject. Next, the participants write until time is called. Usually this is followed with the writer's reading their product. (Example: The topic is Mother Love and the writer has ten minutes to write—then they take turns reading their stories to the group.)

Sometimes poets will be challenged to create on the spot pieces (usually out loud as opposed to writing) for the entertainment of the audience.

This could be a fun activity for your prose writing group too, and it might get the creative juices flowing (if that's what you need.)

CREDENTIALS
(See also Platform)

Showing who you are and why you are the right one to write this piece.

Used especially
when submitting
a non-fiction manuscript.

In non-fiction, credentials and platform are almost interchangeable.

Publishers and agents want to know *how and why* this writer is knowledgeable enough to write about this subject.

If you are a Master Gardner, then you have the credentials and knowledge to write how-to articles or books about certain aspects of gardening or other related subjects, like pruning or even flower arranging, but you probably wouldn't have the information necessary to write about nuclear fission.

Serving up your credentials or platform in a query letter is critical and especially important in proposals. This information could be the tipping point as to whether or not a manuscript is accepted.

CREDITS

The list of people who helped or made a piece possible. Also, information about the places the writer got information for the piece.

Giving credit
where credit is due.

Many non-fiction books list reference materials or participating people in the back of their books. It is a way of saying thank you to people that helped with facts, gave pictures, or shared their knowledge so that this book could be written. Even fiction books sometimes make a list of credits that helped make the story better or more factual.

Example:

In non-fiction books about alligators, the credits could name places and people who showed the author how to capture or even find alligators to study.

In a fictional mystery book about miners, the credits might list the names of those people in the mining business who gave information to the author so that places or a time-line would be correct, or maybe they even let the author go down in a mine for more real-life info.

CRITIQUE/CRITIQUE GROUPS
(See also Feedback)

Persons (singularly or in groups) who will give a writer constructive feedback about their writing.

New writers
can find this
Especially helpful.

Beginning writers learn more easily with constructive feedback from other writers, but don't mistake critique for criticism. Critique means giving suggestions of how to make it better, not an attack on the writer.

Joining a critique group is a very good way to receive this feedback. If the group is made up of people in all stages of writing (published and beginners), they can help each other. A published writer will pick up on formatting and guideline problems, and a beginning writer's questions will refresh the knowledge of the whole group.

Warning: If you give your writing to a spouse for a critique, this is the risk you take: You might get one of two responses: I really like this (because I like you.), or if they say anything negative, even in the vein of helping, it seems too personal. Now that said, some family members might know about writing and be helpful, but if they are not a writer, they may not be the best person to critique your work.

CYBER WRITING
(See also E-books and Blog)

Another name for published on the Internet.

> Internet Blogs, e-books and e-zines . . .
> Another place for your stories.

Writing pieces for the Internet is one way to get published (e-publishing). In the early stages of blogging and on the Internet sites that published stories or articles, the term was *cyber writing*. This term isn't used as much now, having been replaced with terms such as e-books or e-zines, and on-line publishing.

And, it's important to remember that if you have a story or article printed on any Internet site, it is published and you can no longer *sell* first publishing rights. This doesn't mean it can't be published again, but first publishing rights have already been used.

DARK FICTION
(See also Noir Fiction)

Stories from the dark or really unhappy side of life, or maybe about the afterlife.

> Spooky, scary, and ugly
> —oh my!

Books written about wars or police action or about any of the rough side of life could also be called dark fiction. Anything that is not up-lifting or that is meant to show or depict tragedy can be dark fiction too.

And then, the books about vampires and werewolves and devil worshiping are all about the darker side, and some dark fiction can also be called graphic action fiction.

DEADLINES

Deadlines are like a curfew for writers—an exact time that submissions are due at the publisher's or editor's desk.

> Writing to a deadline
> helps some writers.

It would be a very chaotic publishing world if there were no expected times for work to be finished. Trains and buses and airlines run on schedules and so do publishers. In order to get a magazine or newspaper articles into print, authors need to present their finished work at a pre-determined time—a time dictated by the publication. If a writer wants to get a piece published, they will check the guidelines and heed the deadline for submission.

Contests also have submission deadlines, and if you are too late, your piece might not even be considered.

DIALOGUE

Conversations between characters, either spoken, overheard, or just their thoughts.

The he said, she said
part of a story.

Adding dialogue or conversations to your story can further the plot line by adding information or giving explanations of something, or fleshing out the image you want the reader to have about a particular character.

And don't forget that along with the dialogue, the actions while they speak can help describe and define these people that populate your story.

Example:
"Come over here, honey." she said and looked at him, eyelids lowered over her dark, brooding, brown eyes, and then she brushed her overly bleached blond hair off her furrowed brow.

The dialogue is only *"Come over here, Honey"* but part of her description is described in the actions she took while speaking. Not just the words, but showing info about the person while they are speaking is a very effective tool for writers.

DRAFT
(See also Editing)

A manuscript before it is deemed finished is still a draft copy.

> Some writers think
> they are never finished.

    When a writer starts a piece, it is referred to as a draft and continues to be a draft all the while it is being written, Some writers number their drafts and will say "The first (or second or third) draft is finished". This usually means the writer has finished the complete piece but still thinks there is editing to do.

    Draft is a signal word that writers employ to tell others where they are in this process of getting to the finished product.

DREK
(See also Body of Work)

In newspaper and magazine slang, the articles have a beginning or intro, drek or middle, and walk-off or ending part. Drek is the middle portion, or meat of an article.

(These newspaper terms, although not used in newspaper publishing much now, were in a handout at a workshop about writing for a newspaper at a PNWA Writers Conference.)

> Newspaper slang
> for middle stuff.

It may not be widely used any more, but newspapers and their writers have their own slang words that mean special things to their writing. Following this line, news articles have three parts:

The **beginning** or intro (who/what/where),
The **drek** (middle where the story unfolds), and
The **walk-off** (ending, when the story is wrapped up and finished.)

DUMMY COPY
(See also Blueline Copy)

A finished product but probably not the final copy of the book.

Before
the real thing.

After all the editing and after the formatting and after the layouts are all approved then a dummy copy is put together. When this final step is finished and approved, then the book is printed and is ready for distribution.

E-BOOKS/E-PUBLISHING
(See also Cyber Publishing)

Any book or story you put (show and display all the words of and all the chapters of) on the Internet or make available for electronic readers is considered electronic publishing or e-publishing

> Should I present my book
> on my blog?

Several writers have gotten their stories published (or at least recognized) by entering them in contests on the Internet. If the story is displayed for reader consumption, then it is considered published (electronic published). And if a writer has a blog or website and decides to serialize their book for their readers, it is also considered published, so be *aware* that this may use up your first publishing rights.

EDGY FICTION
(See also Action Fiction)

Not shocking or extremely explicit (like murder scenes filled with blood and guts), but right on the edge—and very exciting.

> Showing the reader what happened,
> but not over the edge.

When you write explicit details about a ski accident and describe in detail the bones sticking out of the torn flesh, or if you describe a sex scene in explicit terms, this is going too far for Edgy Fiction (it is gritty fiction.)

However, writing about the skier going out of control and heading for a crash, or the romance that leads the couple to a room and closing the door, that is edgy fiction—right up to the point of being too graphic or gritty.

EDIT/EDITING

Finding punctuation or other things that need fixing in your document is called editing.

Self-editing as you go
or
professional help,
both are good things.

Now that the manuscript is finished, the author will want to go back over the printed words to see if any changes are needed. This is editing. It can be done by the writer, but a professional editor could possibly catch things the writer might overlook.

Self-editing is just a fact of being a writer but when you feel the piece is ready for submission, having another pair of eyes read the manuscript is a good step. Writers tend to not see missing adjectives or conjunctions in their own work. They sometimes read what should be there instead of what really has been written.

Here's a trick for self-editing: Read your words out loud in front of a mirror. It gives the reader the sense that someone is listening. If there are any places you stumble, they should be marked, because maybe your readers would stubble there too and a good writer certainly doesn't want that.

EDITING/MARK-UP COPY
(See also Galley/Galley Proof)

A first copy of a book that is marked up and edited before the final or galley print is made.

Another step
in getting a book ready
to sell.

Before the book is actually printed for distribution to booksellers, it must be looked at for mistakes/typos/errors in pagination, etc. This first copy is called an editing/mark-up copy for just this purpose. One of the many stages a book goes through before the public can finally get it to read.

EDITOR

Publishers employ people who work with manuscripts and/ or a writer can also hire someone to help edit the manuscript. Both of these are called editors and are interested in seeing the manuscript through to publication.

Corrections and changes
for the good of the story.

Before a manuscript is presented to a publisher or agent it should be polished and polished again. Hiring a person that is a professional editor—one that knows what time-line is and understands POV and Voice—is a great help in this polishing process and is really a necessary part before submission.

In the publishing world, there are many publishing positions. A writer's manuscript will probably start out with a junior editor, and then perhaps be passed on to a more senior level editor until it reaches an executive level. At the highest level, the editor takes on the responsibility for getting this book to its final stages (printed and released to the public). However, in small publishing houses, the more hats each editor wears, so it could be only one person/editor who takes a manuscript all the way from first read all the way to production.

EDITORIAL CALENDAR

The publisher's plans and time frame for upcoming books.

When do they plan to publish
your book?

In magazine and newspaper publishing, an editorial calendar is a way to keep track of what and when will be published in each issue. This is especially helpful if a theme is being used (like holiday issues, or bride month, or back to school).

Example:
If a magazine plans to run articles about make-up, it might want to contact make-up companies to do extra advertising in that issue.

In publishing houses these editorial calendars could keep track of when a book is to be printed so that publicity and public appearances can be arranged.

ELEVATOR SPEECH
(See also Blurb)

The art of describing your story/manuscript in a few sentences.

Short and sweet.

This is what an Elevator Speech is:

You are presented with an opportunity to tell an agent or publisher what your book is about (maybe even in an elevator), but you only have the length of time it would take for the elevator to go from the first to the fourth floor.

Three or four sentences are all that is needed to give the gist of the story. If you think you need to tell a whole back story before you can tell the main points, your speech will need lots of work.

Think of it as telling a friend about a movie you saw. You might start by saying "The name of the movie was Slim and Slimmer" but you wouldn't explain that first the lion came on and roared, and then the name of the movie came on, and then the characters were listed—you would get right to the point.

For example you might say, "This movie is about two fat guys that go to a spa for six weeks and have a race to see who can lose the most weight." A short plot explanation.

Then, if the agent or editor is interested after hearing this short synopsis, they will ask questions or ask for more detail.

ENDORSEMENT

Notable people telling readers why they liked a particular book.

You should read this
book because . . .

When you go to a bookstore you pick up a book and perhaps read what is written on the back cover. Also located on the back cover may be excerpts from newspaper reviews or statements from other authors that say what they found interesting in this story/book.

In non-fiction, an endorsement could be made by a school, or organization or foundation that thinks this book will help people better understand what they are about.

EPILOGUE

The final section or last part and comes after the final chapter.

The last words,
so to speak.

At the end of a book, the section (after the last chapter) could be considered an epilogue if it ties up all the loose ends and maybe hints at a sequel to this book.

Another use of an epilogue could be a part revealing what happened to the characters in the future—perhaps ten years later, revealing a happy-ever-after or a look-what-the-consequences-were ending of the story.

EROTICA
(See also Action and Gritty Fiction)

Very explicit love scenes told in great detail.

> Letting it all
> hang out.

There is a market for erotic fiction. It is show-and-tell in a very great detail.

When a writer includes these explicit sexual actions and descriptions in their stories, they should make sure that they submit it to the agents and editors that want to publish this type of work.

EXPOSITION
(See also Narrative Nonfiction)

Providing background and information about a story, its characters, or its setting.

Tells facts

and

gives statements.

Rhetorical comes from the word rhetoric which means the art of communicating. Exposition is one form of rhetoric.

Rhetorical Modes of Speech or writing is a big phrase that simply means giving facts to the audience (in this case the reader).

There are four common modes:

Exposition: The purpose of exposition is to provide some background and inform the readers about the plot, character, setting, and theme of the essay or story. This includes speeches and the background of characters.

Argumentation: Usually means debate.

Description: Primarily used to tell the reader what people look like, and about settings.

Narration: The narrator tells the story with very little character chit chat.

Seldom do you hear the word Rhetorical Mode used but if you do, you'll have a start at understanding what they mean.

F & G COPY

A term used for a manuscript before it is published, such as picture books. Much like an ARC (advance reader copy).

Publishing slang
Meaning
folded and gathered.

F&G's is a publishing term that means (roughly) un-cut, large sheets of paper, which later get folded and cut to make the book. It could be created when you get a picture book published.

An author could be sent an F&G to proof before publishers do a whole print run or possibly as an advance copy for reviewers.

Each publisher has their own way of doing this part of the process.

FABLE
(See also Fantasy and Folklore)

Stories told, usually in order to deliver a moral lesson.

Do-it-this-way
lessons.

Stories like fairy tales are a good example of the tales that were used for teaching what expected actions were to be taken (like manners and doing good works) in a given situation. These stories are not necessarily just for children, but as they were handed down through generations, they become more entertainment than teaching tools.

FACTOID

A word or statement presented as a fact, but with no real backup confirmation.

Maybe it's true,
and
maybe it's not.

Lots of fiction writers use factoids. These statements are accepted as truth but are they really true?

If you write about vampires, there are many facts that are accepted by the reader that if put to the test of realism would be suspect. This is also true of some historical novels. Facts may be distorted to fit the story line.

Example:
Bonaparte was light on his feet as he danced with his mistress. (Whereas the fact may be that Bonaparte hated dancing and this never would have happened, and maybe he didn't have a mistress.)

FAIR USE
(See also Copyright)

A law governing copyright.

Limitations and expectation.

A story automatically belongs to its writer. If the writer sells this story, they are selling the copyright—the right for it to be printed. The copyright law sets forth rules on how this copyright can be used. Fair use means this story can be used as expected with the limitations that are laid out in the contract.

Example:
A magazine buys a story from an author and the author expects it will be printed *only one time* in the magazine as set out in the contract they signed. However, if the magazine then prints it in another of their publications or in an anthology without the author's permission, they are abusing the fair use provision of the copyright law.

It works the other way too: If a magazine buys a story they have the reasonable expectation that the author will not be selling it to other publications without notification.

This also applies to incorporating another's copyrighted material into your work without giving credit to the originating author.

An author should also be aware that outside the United States there also exists the same laws but they may be called by other names such as Fair Dealing and Common Law Usage.

FANTASY
(See also Speculative Fiction and Science Fiction)

A genre that uses magic and supernatural elements.

> Maybe sorcerers
> and flying dragons?

Imagination is a wonderful tool for the writer. Some have conjured up imaginative worlds using wizards and flying animals and people appearing and disappearing at will, or even whole worlds that are outside of what is actually known.

This is the genre named FANTASY.

FEEDBACK
(See also Critique)

Suggestions and critique of a written piece so that a writer can make it better.

Feedback or critique
should never be personal.

After a writer has made a piece (or even part of his piece) as good as they think it can be, then it's time for feedback.

Many writers belong to critique groups. These like-minded people will be able to give constructive suggestions for making the piece stronger and better. Usually these groups give both positive and even negative comments, but the remarks are never directed toward the author.

Sometimes, if a submission is rejected, the editor or agent will write a note saying why—this is *valuable feedback* from a professional.

Example:
Member of the group says: "I don't understand how the protagonist got to the house." (This probably means that the action isn't clear.) A wrong critique would be "You always leave out how people get from one place to another." (Personal attacks on the author are of no help to making the writing better.)

If a writer gets nothing but negative feedback, it might be a signal that rewriting is needed—clarification of facts or maybe just a time-line correction. Writers should pay attention to all feedback, both negative and positive. After all, these are potential readers and if they are confused then your reader might possibly be too.

FICTION

Stories that are not true, even if based on fact.

> Good story,
> but made up.

   Stories that are told or written from the imagination of the author are called fiction. They could be based on a true story (a nonfiction happening), but all the facts, conversations, character descriptions, and maybe even the time lines are made up by the author.

<u>EXAMPLE:</u>
   Fact: Man walks on the moon
   Fiction: Shelia took her first step onto the moon's surface
      and felt the fine dust move beneath her bare toes.

FIRST TIME RIGHTS
(See also Copyright)

The publisher gets the exclusive right to publish a piece for the first time but must get permission if they want to print it again.

Only once.

When a contract is signed by an author to publish their piece, it is important that the author understand which rights they are assigning (selling). Usually <u>First Time Rights</u> is what the contract will state; however having a lawyer read the contract before you sign it is a good idea.

If the contract should say <u>All Rights</u>, this means movie rights, serial rights, and other publishing and advertising rights and the author should be *very* aware of what they are signing away.

FLASHBACKS

Almost a backstory but told by remembering.

Remember
when?

Using flashbacks is a useful tool for writers and a good way to get information to the reader. It can be an interjected scene that takes the reader and story back in time from the current point in the story.

EXAMPLE: (This is a flashback moment.)

And he leaned forward and kissed her and then he held her face in his hands. She smiled and . . .

(New Chapter)

They met in a strange way, almost missing the opportunities that lay ahead. He was about to board the plane and she was just helping her grand-mother . . .

FOLKLORE
(See also Myths)

Stories, tales, and legends from the past.

> Most fairy tales
> are based on folklore.

Stories like the ones told around a campfire and then repeated from generation to generation are considered folklore. And so are the dances that tell a story (Native American's and some African tribes are an example of this action).

These legends and stories can be of wrong doing or of great adventures from a past generation, culture, century or even just a past childhood, and can be considered folklore.

FONT

When using the computer, the shape and size of letters (the type) in the words is referred to as the font or font size.

> Size and kind
> counts here.

For submission purposes (when you're ready to send your piece out with hopes of getting published), the preferred font size is 12, and the name of the font should be Times New Roman. If you have other formatting questions look for the book *Formatting & Submitting Your Manuscript* by Chuck Sambuchino.

Computer users know there are many, many fonts (types of print) to choose from, and you as a writer can use any one of them you like, however when you are ready to submit, consult and follow the guidelines for the best results.

FOOTER
(See also Header)

On the page generated by a computer, there is the capability of adding information so it will show up on the bottom of the page. This space is called a footer.

> Repeating info
> at the
> bottom of the page.

Footers are at the bottom of the computer-generated page and can hold page numbers or foot notes, or reference information.

Some submission guidelines ask for page numbers to be placed at the bottom of the page (in the footer), but the usual submission guidelines state page numbers and other information (author name and name of piece) should be in the header—the space at the top of the page.

As always, check the guidelines for the submission requirements. They will state where the publisher expects to see page numbers, name of author, and name of piece.

FOOT NOTE

Information adding interest and pertaining to the words written above.

More info

on the bottom

of each page.

Foot notes are usually reference information showing where a statement was garnered from, or from which publication a statement or statistic was taken. It gives the reader more information. It may show up in the footer (bottom of the computer generated page) or just at the bottom of the typed page.

FOREWORD

(See also Introduction, Forward, Prologue, Preface, and Proem)

An introduction to a book, but it's usually *not* written by the author.

A setup for
the rest of the story.

In non-fiction, you might find another authority on the subject of the book has written an introduction. Sometimes it's a praising piece, but it usually presents another (short) view of this same theme/subject. For example, on a book about exploring Africa, the intro might be by another well known explorer saying they enjoyed this book and maybe pointing out parts of particular interest. ("I particularly enjoyed the part in Chapter 10 about the monkey that raided the larder and then shared with the children.")

In fiction, the starting section is usually called a Prologue or a Preface instead of a Foreword and is usually used to set up the story line of the book or to give some backstory information to the reader. (In fiction, a Foreword could be present but it is probably going to be written by a fellow author that says how much they like the story or stories written by the author.)

Warning:

Don't let *foreword* (note the E in the middle of the word*)*, get mixed up with *forward* as in "forward march". They are not interchangeable in meaning (as you can see.)

FORMAT

How your writing is laid out on the page—margins, spacing, etc.

Arranging your story.

How you put your words on a page are almost as important as what the words mean.

When you are submitting to a publisher (or agents or contests), there are certain ways they like to receive the pages and the guidelines will tell you how they want your manuscript laid out. This is called the format. If they do not specify how they want it formatted or if they ask you to follow general guidelines for submission then they usually mean the following:

General rules for formatting a page are:
- 1" Margins all around (Top, Bottom, both right and left sides)
- Times New Roman Font (This is the name of a particular computer font)
- 12 point font (this is the size of the printed letters/words).
- Double space between lines
- 8-1/2" x 11" inch paper size
- White paper (commonly called copy or printer paper).
- Writer's name, name of piece and page number in upper right corner of each page.

FORWARD

To continue in your line of travel as in the direction "Forward march!"

A command meaning
"go."

A common mistake is using the word *forward* when you mean the part of the book before the story starts. This is a *foreword*—words that go before the story.

Watch carefully for this problem when you proofread your piece.

FREELANCE

A writer that works for a company or publisher on a contractual basis as opposed to being an employee of that company.

Paid by the piece

maybe?

A freelance writer can write on many subjects and can submit articles to several magazines or publications but is only paid for the piece that is 'bought for publication'.

Sometimes the publisher will pay by the word or sometimes by the piece but they probably do not consider the freelance writer as an employee.

And as in every statement there are exceptions: Many freelance writers are contributors to a publication on a regular basis and are even given assignments, but they are still not considered employees in the regular sense of the word. They are considered contractors.

FRESH VOICE

A new and different way of writing a story.

An original
take on a plot.

All writers are told that there are no new stories, just different ways of telling them, and a fresh voice means just that. Think of how many stories mimic Cinderella—girl falls in love with a seemingly unattainable man and in spite of these beginnings, they do get together.

Another old plot but new story is *The Notebook* by Nicholas Sparks, in which a poor working guy falls for rich girl.

FRONT LIST

In the publishing world, newly published books (less than a year ago), are called front list books.

> In the front
> of the
> catalog.

The term front list books originated from the practice of publishers issuing catalogs (for sales purposes), featuring their books. The catalogs are typically issued twice a year and usually feature a photo of the cover art for the book, together with press material describing the book and its author. This is a way of telling buyers what is newly published (in the front of the catalog), and also, which older published books are still available.

FRONT MATTER
(See also Back Matter)

All printed matter in a book that precedes the proper start of the book/story.

Maybe a foreword or . . . ?

The title page, the copyright page, the table of contents, the foreword or dedication, and the preface to the story are all considered Front Matter—pages that come before the actual book/story starts.

So logically, all the pages that come after the book/story is finished are called the back matter. This could include author info, other books by this author, glossary of terms, or research info.

GALLEY/GALLEY PROOF
(See also ARC)

The preliminary copy of the final version of a manuscript being printed is called a galley print or galley proof.

First preview
of a
published book.

A galley proof is the printed copy of your book that serves as the copy sent to be reviewed by editors, proofreaders and maybe the author. They may come in an uncut, unbound or even an electronic version for the purpose of making it free of mistake—no extra commas or misspelled words, and it may also be used as a promotional or review copy.

Galley proofs are so named because in the days of hand-set type, the printer would set letters/type into the metal trays (a galley) and then secure them in place by tightening the screws of the box. These would be used to print a limited number of copies for editing. The typesetter would eventually receive the edits/corrections, rearrange the type, and then print the final copy.

GAY LIT
(See also Niche Books)

Books written for and sometimes by a member of the gay community. These fiction books are usually about relationships, much as chick lit and guy lit books are.

A specific topic

for

specific readers.

These niche books are usually books written on a specific topic or for a specific group. Chick Lit, Guy Lit and Gray Lit are examples of niche books, and so are Gay Lit books.

Gay Lit is usually fiction about gay relationships (getting into one or getting rid of one).

Some non-fiction books are in this sub-genre too and feature travel spots, organizations and other topics.

GEEZER BOOKS
(See also Niche Books)

Geezer books are not necessarily written by old guys, but the characters will certainly be from the mature generation.

> Older characters
> can be
> very interesting.

Unlike most niche books—books aimed at a specific audience—geezer books can be of interest to a wider audience than just these mature older characters (usually men.)

If a character is strong and carries a good story, tween readers all the way up to gray lit readers will enjoy the story. *Old Man of the Sea* by Ernest Hemingway, could have been a geezer book if written in today's market.

GENERAL ACTION
(See also Action Fiction)

Any movement or action in a fiction book that furthers the story can be called general action.

> Moving people
> and cars and
> whatever.

Details about such things as a car race, deep sea fishing trip, or a couple on a hiking trip in the Amazon could be for all ages to enjoy and is called general action. However, when the actions becomes explicit—like gun fights that describe blood squirting or car crashes with severed limbs—then this is more edgy or gritty, depending on how explicit the details get.

Edgy Action Fiction: Details written about the bleeding after the crash but doesn't describe the smashing of the drivers head on the windshield, or a description of the animal attack, or details about a couple's ski trip that may show the action of tangled skis and the aftermath confusion would all be edgy—action on the edge of having the details written in a too graphic or realistic way.

Gritty Action Fiction: Explicit details about everything, and written with a specific audience in mind. The actions are *very graphic* descriptions that include explicit details of such things as knife wounds being inflicted and how they look and feel with the blood dripping, etc., or African adventures with animal attacks, or a ski trips that end with bones sticking out of the leg.

GENRE
(See also Audience)

The category that a manuscript fits into.

Who's your audience?

One of the first questions asked of a writer when they are submitting their writing for publication is *What is the genre*. What the agent or publisher wants to know is if this is a mystery, romance, memoir, sci-fi, or something else. All writers should know where their piece fits—which genre it is in.

The formal definition of genre means to sort by specific interests, but often these literary works fit into multiple genres by way of borrowing and recombining the definitions of each category.

Writings usually fit into a main genre such as Romance, Mystery, Sci-fi/Fantasy, or Memoirs, and to confuse things further, these general heading also include sub-headings and here are some examples:

(There could be some sub-subgenres not listed here, but this list may still help you determine where your piece might fit.)

Romance:
Chick-Lit: often humorous, romantic adventures of single working women in their twenties and thirties.

Christian: romances in which both hero and heroine are devout Christians, typically focused on a chaste courtship, and mentioning sex only after marriage.

Contemporary: a romance using modern characters and true-to-life settings.

Erotica: also called *romantica*—a romance in which the bedroom doors have been flung open and sexual scenes are described in candid and explicit language.

Glitz/Glamor: focused on the jet-set elite and celebrity-like characters.

Historical: a romance taking place in a recognizable historical period.

Multicultural: a romance centered on non-Caucasian characters (could be African-American or Hispanic or Asian).

Paranormal: involving some sort of supernatural element, ranging widely to include science fiction/fantasy aspects such as time travel, monsters or psychic abilities.

Romantic Comedy: a romance focused on humor, ranging from screwball antics to witty repartee.

Romantic Suspense: a novel in which an admirable heroine is pitted against some evil force (but in which the romantic aspect still maintains priority).

Sensual: based on the sensual tension between hero and heroine, including sizzling sex scenes.

Spicy: a romance in which married characters (or perhaps unmarried partners/characters) work to resolve their problems.

Sweet: a romance centered on a virgin heroine with a story line containing little or no sex.

Young Adult: written with the teenage audience in mind, with a suitably low level of sexual content.

Horror:

Child in Peril: involving the abduction and/or persecution of a child.

Comic Horror: horror stories that either spoof horror conventions, or that mix the gore with dark humor.

Creepy Kids: horror tale in which children, often under the influence of dark forces, begin to turn against the adults.

Dark Fantasy: a horror story with supernatural and fantasy elements.

Dark Mystery/Noir: inspired by hardboiled detective tales, set in an urban underworld of crime and moral ambiguity.

Erotic Vampire: a horror tale making the link between sexuality and vampires, but with more emphasis on graphic description and violence.

Fabulist: derived from *fable*, an ancient tradition in which objects, animals, or forces of nature are anthropomorphized in order to deliver a moral lesson.

Gothic: a traditional form depicting the encroachment of the Middle Ages upon the eighteenth century enlightenment, filled with images of decay and ruin, and episodes of imprisonment and persecution.

Hauntings: a classic form centering on possession by ghosts, demons, or poltergeists, particularly in some sort of structure.

Historical: scary horror tales set in a specific and recognizable period of history.

Magical Realism: a genre inspired by Latin-American authors in which extraordinary forces or creatures pop into otherwise normal, real-life settings.

Psychological: a story based on the disturbed human psyche; often exploring insane, altered realities and featuring a human monster with horrific but not supernatural aspects.

Quiet Horror: subtly written horror that uses atmosphere and mood rather than graphic description to create fear and suspense. (Alfred Hitchcock was adept at this in his movies.)

Religious: horror that makes use of religious icons and mythology, especially the angels and demons derived from Dante Alighieri's *Inferno* and John Milton's *Paradise Lost*.

Science-Fiction Horror: sci-fi with a darker, more violent twist; often revolving around alien invasions, mad scientists, or experiments gone wrong.

Splatter: a fairly new, extreme style of horror that cuts right to the gore.

Supernatural Menace: a horror tale in which the rules of normal existence don't apply, often featuring ghosts, demons, vampires and werewolves.

Techno Horror: stories featuring technology that has run amok, venturing increasingly into the expanding domain of computers, cyberspace, and genetic engineering.

Weird Tales: inspired by the magazine of the same name, a more traditional form featuring strange and uncanny events, like *The Twilight Zone*.

Young Adult: horror aimed at a teen market, often with heroes the same age, or slightly older than the reader.

Zombie: tales featuring dead people who return to commit mayhem on the living.

Thriller/Suspense:

Action: a story that often features a race against the clock, lots of violence, and an obvious antagonist.

Comic: a thriller played for laughs, whether through a spoof of the genre or wisecracking interplay between protagonists.

Conspiracy: a thriller in which the hero battles a large, powerful group whose true intent only he recognizes.

Crime: a story focused on the commission of a crime, often from the point of view of the criminal(s).

Disaster: a story in which Mother Nature herself is the antagonist, in the form of a hurricane, earthquake or some other natural menace.

Eco-Thriller: a story in which the hero battles some ecological calamity, and often has to also fight the people responsible for creating that calamity.

Erotic: a thriller in which sex plays a major role.

Espionage: the classic international spy novel, which is enjoying a resurgence with one important change: where spies used to battle enemy spies, they now battle terrorists.

Forensic: a thriller featuring the work of medical and forensic experts whose involvement often puts their own lives at risk.

Historical: tales taking place in a specific and recognizable historic period.

Horror: a story generally featuring some monstrous villain in which fear and violence plays a major part, complete with graphic descriptions.

Legal: a thriller in which a lawyer confronts enemies outside as well as inside the courtroom, generally putting his own life at risk.

Medical: a story featuring medical personnel who may be battling a legitimate medical threat such as a world-wide virus, or the illegal or immoral use of medical technology.

Military: stories featuring a military protagonist, often working behind enemy lines or as part of a specialized force.

Police Procedural: a crime thriller that follows the police as they work their way through a case.

Political Intrigue: a thriller in which the hero must ensure the stability of the government that employs him.

Psychological: a suspenseful thriller in which the conflict between the characters is mental and emotional rather than physical—until an often violent resolution.

Romantic: a thriller in which the protagonists are romantically involved.

Supernatural: a thriller in which the character(s) has supernatural powers.

Technological: a thriller in which technology is usually central to the plot.

Science Fiction/Fantasy

Alternate History or Historical Fiction: speculative fiction that changes the accepted account of actual historical events, often featuring a profound "what if?" premise.

Arthurian Fantasy: reworking of the legend of King Arthur and the Knights of the Round Table.

Bangsian Fantasy: stories speculating on the afterlives of famous people.

Biopunk: a blend of film noir and post-modern elements used to describe an underground peopled by a pessimistic or negative biotech society.

Children's Fantasy: a kinder, gentler style of fantasy aimed at very young readers. (Think fairy tales.)

Comic: fantasy or science fiction that spoofs the conventions of the genre, or the conventions of society.

Cyberpunk: stories featuring tough outsiders in a high-tech near-future where computers have produced major changes in society.

Dark Fantasy: tales that focus on the nightmarish underbelly of magic, venturing into the violence.

Dystopian: stories that portray a bleak future world.

Erotic: fantasy tales that focus on sexuality.

Game-Related Fantasy: tales with plots and characters similar to fantasy, but based on a specific role-playing game like Dungeons and Dragons.

Hard Science Fiction: tales in which real present-day science is logically extrapolated to the future.

Heroic Fantasy: stories of war and its heroes; much like military science fiction.

High/Epic Fantasy: tales with an emphasis on the fate of an entire race or nation; often featuring a young *nobody hero* battling an ultimate evil.

Historical: speculative fiction taking place in a recognizable historical period.

Mundane Sci-Fi: a movement that spurns fanciful concepts like wormholes and faster-than-light travel for stories based on scientific knowledge as it actually exists.

Military SF: war stories that extrapolate existing military technology and tactics into the future.

Mystery Sci-Fi: a cross-genre blend that can be either a sci-fi tale with a central mystery or a classic whodunit with sci-fi elements.

Mythic Fiction: stories inspired, or modeled after classic myths, legends, and fairy tales.

New Age: a category of speculative fiction that deals with occult subjects such as astrology, psychic phenomena, spiritual healing, UFOs, or mysticism.

Post-Apocalyptic: stories of life on Earth after an apocalypse, focusing on the human struggle to survive.

Romance: speculative fiction in which romance plays a key part.

Religious: stories centered on theological ideas, and protagonists/heroes who are ruled by their religious beliefs.

Science Fantasy: a blend of facts in which fantasy is supported by scientific or pseudo-scientific explanations.

Social Sci-Fi: tales that focus on how characters react to their environments, including social satire.

Soft Sci-Fi: tales based on the more subjective, softer sciences, including psychology, sociology, anthropology, etc.

Space Opera: a traditional good guys/bad guys faceoff with lots of action and larger-than-life characters.

Spy-Fi: tales of espionage with sci-fi parts, especially the use of high-tech gadgetry.

Steampunk: a specific type of alternate history (for example, characters in Victorian England have access to 20th century technology).

Superheroes: stories featuring characters endowed with superhuman strengths or abilities.

Sword and Sorcery: a classic genre often set in the medieval period and more concerned with immediate physical threats than high or heroic goals.

Thriller Sci-Fi: a story that takes on the classic world-at-risk, cliffhanger elements of a thriller.

Time Travel: stories based on the concept of moving forward or backward in time, often delving into the existence of parallel worlds.

Urban Fantasy: a fantasy tale in which magical powers and characters appear in an otherwise normal modern context.

Vampire: variations on the classic vampire legend, and recently taking on sexual and romantic variations.

Wuxia: fantasy tales set within the martial arts traditions and philosophies of Asia.

Young Adult: speculative fiction aimed at a teenage audience; often featuring a hero the same age or slightly older than the reader.

Mystery/Crime:

Amateur Detective: a mystery solved by an amateur, who generally has some profession or affiliation that provides ready access to information about the crime.

Child in Peril: a mystery involving the abduction or persecution of a child.

Classic Whodunit: a crime that is solved by a detective, from the detective's point of view, with all clues available to the reader.

Comic (Bumbling Detective): a mystery played for laughs, often featuring a detective who is grossly unskilled (but often solves the crime anyway, owing to tremendous good luck).

Cozy: a mystery that usually takes place in a small town where all the suspects are present and familiar with one another, except the detective, who may sometimes be an eccentric outsider.

Courtroom Drama: a mystery that takes place through the justice system; often the efforts of a defense attorney to prove the innocence of his client by finding the real culprit.

Dark Thriller: a mystery that ventures into the fear factor and graphic violence of the horror genre.

Espionage: the international spy novel, perhaps based less on action than on solving a puzzle. Today's stories are less focused on the traditional enemy spies and more on terrorists.

Forensic: a mystery solved through a forensics lab and featuring much detail on medical and scientific procedure.

Heists and Capers: an antihero genre that focuses on the planning and execution of a crime, told from the criminal's perspective.

Historical: a mystery that takes place in a specific, recognizable period of history, with much emphasis on the details of the setting.

Inverted: a story in which the reader knows "whodunit," but the suspense arises from watching the detective figure it out.

Locked Room: a mystery in which the crime is apparently committed under impossible circumstances but eventually elicits a rational explanation.

Medical: generally involving a medical threat, perhaps a viral epidemic, or the illegitimate use of medical technology (like cloning).

Police Procedural: a crime solved from the perspective of the police, following detailed, real-life procedures.

Private Detective: stories focused on the independent snoop-for-hire. These have changed from tough-guy/hard-boiled detectives to the more professional operators of today.

Psychological Suspense: mysteries focused on the intricacies of the crime and what motivated the perpetrator to commit them.

Romantic: a mystery in which the crime-solvers also encounter romance.

Techno-thriller: a spinoff from the traditional thriller mystery, with an emphasis on high technology.

Thriller: a suspense mystery with a wider, often international scope, and lots of action.

Woman in Jeopardy: focuses on a woman put into peril by a crime, and her struggles to overcome or outwit the perpetrator/bad guys.

Young Adult: a story aimed at a teenage audience; the hero detective is generally the same age or slightly older than the reader, pursuing criminals that are generally less violent but often just as scary as those in adult mysteries.

GHOST WRITER

A writer who writes books, articles, stories, and/or a biography that is officially credited to another person.

> You write it,
> however . . .

Celebrities and others too will sometimes want to hire a ghostwriter (perhaps someone outside their business or social circle), to write or maybe to edit their personal stories or other written materials. Sometimes these brought-in-writers will not be acknowledged; however, this is the nature of ghost writing.

These writers may also be involved in the research for, or maybe just edit/fix of an already written piece (like re-writing a book). The ghost writer will be paid but not have the normal publicity that goes with the publishing of this project. Writing a famous person's memoirs could a part of ghost writing too.

Ghostwriting can be very lucrative, and these special writers are increasingly in demand and needed.

GLITZY ROMANCE
(See also Genre/Romance)

Stories told about the romantic escapades of movie stars, high rollers, or globe-trotters that show their extravagant lifestyles.

Silver, gold,
and
diamonds abound.

The glamorous life styles of the rich and famous make for glitzy reading, and if you add a romance you'll be writing a glitzy romance story. In these stories exclusive resorts or mansions are normal settings and descriptions of the characters' expensive designer finery, parties, or escapade only adds to the glitz.

GRAY LIT

Gray lit is a subgenre in romance—romantic escapades of the mature kind.

Never too old for
romance.

Romance can happen at any stage of your life, and getting to the senior chapter does not lessen the human desire for companionship. If you are writing a romance and the main characters are retired or even just past fifty years of age, then you're writing a gray lit. These stories about mature love and mature people are not only read by seniors, they are popular with romance readers across the board.

GRITTY ACTION FICTION
(See also Action Fiction)

Explicit details written to paint a vivid picture of an event.

All the real
and
maybe ugly details.

This genre includes *very graphic* descriptions of an action—blood and guts galore. For example, an incident where someone was attacked by a dog would include a detailed description of all the blood and screaming and maybe painful aftermath.

This type of book is written with a specific audience in mind.

GUIDELINES

Rules set out for submissions of a manuscript.

Submission time is not
a time to break the rules.

When a manuscript is ready for a publisher or agent to see, a writer needs to be aware of the guidelines (rules this publisher or agent has set forth) for submission.

If no guidelines are issued, it is good to follow this generally accepted list:
 1" margins all around (top/bottom/left/right)
 Indented paragraphs
 Size of type (Times New Roman-12 pointt is preferred)
 Double spaced lines
 Title of piece and author name (usually in the top right-corner of each page)
 Manuscript Page numbers(usually in the top right-corner of each page)

Example:
 My Plate Is Full (title of piece)
 John Doe (author's name)
 Page 1 (page numbers of manuscript)

If you are submitting to a magazine or newspaper, those guidelines will be individually set out and they may also tell you what content the publication expects. They may even indicate the audience this piece should be written for, and certainly the number of words they expect.

If a writer is in doubt, a request for guidelines is very reasonable and better safe than sorry. Manuscripts are frequently rejected just because they are not submitted in the usual, prescribed and expected way—following the guidelines.

GUY LIT

Fiction written with the male interest in mind, and usually contains romance.

> Light reading, like chick lit,
> but for guys.

Romance fiction is not only for women. Men like to read about relationships and the romantic chase, even if they don't usually admit it.

Guy Lit, much like chick lit or gray lit all follow the path of looking for that special someone, and perhaps finding that person and then the happily-ever-after ending.

HARDBACK BOOK
(See also Softcover Book)

Those lovely books with the stiff, hard covers and perhaps a protective paper cover with a picture of the author and a story blurb are called hardback books.

> Hard-covers,
> hard-bound, and
> hard-back reads.

A book is considered hardbacked, hardcovered or hardbound if the covers are rigid and protective—typically of cardboard covered with cloth or heavy paper. With some vintage books, leather is used.

The spine will be rigid and glued in place or it may even be stitched.

HARD COPY

This is a computer term that means words and stories printed on paper as opposed to being in a file on a computer, disc, or thumb-drive.

Your story
after you print it out.

Most writers now use a computer instead of a typewriter or writing in long hand, although all three are certainly still used by some.

When using a computer, the term *hard copy* means a printed out copy. Before it is printed it is called a file or document and as such can sometimes be used in submissions (if the guidelines permit e-mail submissions), but many publishers, editors, and agents prefer a hard copy of your manuscript. Again, the guidelines will tell you how to submit.

HEADER
(See also Footer)

When writing on the computer, the space above the text is called a header.

A place to put
page info and maybe more.

Manuscripts that are ready for submission to a publisher should include certain information on each page. To achieve this (when using a computer), writers can use the feature called the header. In this header, the information should be the title of the piece, the author's name, and the page number unless the guidelines set out by the publisher asks for something different.

Always follow the guidelines.

HEN LIT
(See also Gray Lit)

Romantic stories in which the main characters are mature women and men, well past their twenties and thirties.

Stories about and for
the more mature FEMALE audience.

Beach reads (short romantic novels) are mostly about romance and the happy ending. Hen lit, just like gray lit involves women (who are mature---past the 50 year mark usually), women seeking/finding/accidently finding an interesting mate. This mate might be temporary or more long-term, but the story always contains romantic elements (yes, even if it is a mystery.)

HERO/HEROINE

The good guys and gals in stories can be called heroes and heroines

Good GUY,
and probably
the main character.

Male (hero) and female (heroine) characters in a work of fiction are usually the main characters and the reader is meant to like them.

Protagonists (the bad guy) could also be a main character but usually not a hero or heroine (unless a change takes place during the story).

HOLIDAY DEADLINES
(See also Deadlines)

Magazines and newspapers usually have very early deadlines for holiday issues, sometimes as far out as six months.

> Holidays always take more
> time to prepare for.

Holiday publications are the ultimate theme-oriented publication because most of the submissions (even the advertising) are slanted toward this particular holiday. In order to get everything into place, publishers usually require a longer lead time (a holiday deadline), far ahead of the publishing date. Newspapers may ask for a submission a month in advance, and magazines may ask for submissions as far ahead as six months in advance of publication.

If you want to write holiday pieces, consult the guidelines of the publication, and if it isn't specified in the general guidelines, contact the magazine or newspaper editor for a deadline date.

It is important for a writer to know deadline information.

HOOK

The first words of any piece are meant to draw the reader into the story. This is a hook—something to make the reader want to read more.

> Catch a reader
> quickly!

When a reader picks up a new book at the store, they might read the blurb on the back of the book (a short synopsis), but more than likely they will open the book to the first chapter and read a few lines. These first lines are the writer's chance to draw the perspective reader into the story and make them want to read/buy the book, thereby hooking the reader on the story.

Sometimes the whole first paragraph is the hook but the quicker a writer can get the reader interested in the story, the better.

ILLUSTRATED

A written prose that contains pictures related to the story is considered illustrated.

Children's books
are often enhanced
with pictures or drawings.

Sketches, photos, or colored drawings interspersed among the written word can help tell the story, especially in children's books, but even in adult fiction, more and more books contain graphics. Both fiction and non-fiction can use illustrations (pictures or drawings) to further the understanding of the story or piece.

An illustration may be a drawing of symbols talked about in the story, or a photograph of the site of the story, or maybe a picture of a character in the story. As long as it helps the reader understand and enjoy the piece, illustrations can be part of the manuscript.

ILLUSTRATORS

The artists and photographers who furnish pictures for books and magazines are the illustrators. They help to tell the stories.

Picture makers.

The people who draw the pictures and sketches and take the photos for any given story are the illustrators. Children's books especially utilize this service.

Warning: Unless you are the illustrator *and* the writer, most publishers prefer to furnish the illustrator for your books (but of course, exceptions are made).

INNW
Pronounced In-Wah

Slang acronym for If Not Now, When?

Well, when?

This bunch of letters (pronounced IN-WAH) has been used by teachers and mentors for many years and seems to apply to writers especially. How many times have you heard someone who professes to be a writer say, "I don't have time now" or "I'll get to that soon" or "It's not the right time for me to write that now". Well, *if not now, when* is the question.

For a writer, setting goals is important, very helpful, and necessary for getting projects done. It's a must to get the kind of production out of yourself that you need/want.

So ask yourself INNW? and get started.

INDEX
(See also Appendix, Bibliography, and Back Matter)

Listing of chapters, names, places, or topics with corresponding page numbers to indicate where to find the desired information.

Where to find it.

In a nonfiction book, how to find the desired information is important, so a list can be included (usually in the back of the book) to tell the reader where to find what he is looking for. This index is also included in what's called the back matter.

INTERVIEW

Talking to someone to get information about a specific event or topic is an interview.

> Getting the
> facts straight.

During a person-to-person interview, you can ask questions and get impressions that just reading a statement can't really give you. An interview can help fill in those unknown parts about a happening or a person, and make for interesting non-fiction reading in magazines or newspapers. Impressions of the subject during an interview can add interest to the written piece.

Fiction can also benefit from interviews and getting facts—then using fictitious names and maybe places, the author could turn the story of this interview into a novel.

INTRODUCTION
(See also Foreword and Proem)

At the beginning of some books, both fiction and nonfiction, the author might write an introduction to the story or give information.

Sort of foreshadowing
the
upcoming subject.

Introductions can be written by the author of the book or by someone else who is an authority on the subject about to be presented. Even fiction can be enhanced by an expert.

Example:
In a fiction book about escaping from a volcano, the intro could be from an expert on volcanoes and how they happen or what conditions precede an eruption. This knowledge would give information to the reader that could enhance the story or the reading.

IRC
(See also SASE/SAP/SAE)

An acronym for International Return Coupon. These are used for postage when mailing to foreign countries.

To ensure a reply

or,

the return of a manuscript.

European publishers (or most publishers or agents outside the USA) will return your manuscript if you (the author) furnish return postage, which is called an International Return Coupon (an IRC).

Most post offices in the US have these on-site for your use. If you are sending queries to anywhere outside of the United States Postal Service, an IRC (International Return Coupon) will be needed. The post office can explain it to you in detail.

Warning: _Do not_ glue or stick the IRC to anything. Simply attach it with a clip on the inside of the package.

ISBN

These letters stand for International Standard Book Number. It is an identifying numbering system.

Identity marking
of a
published book.

An ISBN looks like this: ISBN 1-55105-083-8 and this is what the different parts of the number mean:

The *1*, *A*, or *O* in the first position indicates that the book was published in an English-speaking country. (Other countries have other identifying numbers or letters.)

55105 is the identification number of the publisher

83 identifies the specific title and edition

8 is the check digit (comes from a formula used for identification purposes by the International ISBN Agency and assigned to each set of nine numbers).

An ISBN is assigned to each commercial book edition (except reprintings), as an identifier. The ISBN is thirteen digits long if assigned after January 1, 2007, and ten digits long if assigned before that date. A block of numbers is assigned to each publisher.

This system was created by Gordon Foster, emeritus professor of statistics at Trinity College in Dublin for booksellers and stationer W.H. Smith and others in 1966.

The ten-digit ISBN format was developed by the International Organization for Standardization (ISO). A central secretariat in Geneva, Switzerland, coordinates the system.

For more details see
wikipedia.org/International_Standard_Book_Number.

Something of Interest:
Other organizations also use a standardized numbering system to keep track of their products:

ISRC (International Standard Recording Code)
ISWC (International Standard Musical Work Code)
ISWN (International Standard Wine Number)

ISSN

Identifying numbers for periodical publications.

Another finder.

An International Standard Serial Number (ISSN) is a unique, eight-digit number used to identify a print or electronic periodical publication (eISSN). Periodicals published in both print and electronic form may have two ISSNs: a print ISSN (pISSN) and an electronic ISSN (eISSN).

The ISSN system was first drafted as an ISO in 1971 and published as ISO 3297 in 1975. The ISO (International Standards Organization) subcommittee is responsible for this system.

JOURNALING

Writing your thoughts and activities into a notebook or a single document on a regular basis is called journaling.

Sort of like
our mothers'
diaries.

Writers can benefit from the act of journaling, making notes about your daily activities and thoughts. Keeping a journal of one's submission history can also be quite handy as a reference tool. Don't forget to include notes identifying the submitted piece, the date of submission, the publisher/editor/ agent submitted to, what rights were asked for, what payment was offered, any appropriate deadline information, and then the rejection or acceptance letters.

Your Journal is also a good place to try out different styles of writing such as POV (Should you write in first person as though you were talking, or third person as if you were telling the story?) And the biggest argument of all for journaling is that writers must write, even between novels or stories for publication.

And remember:

Writers get ideas from so many places; from activities around them, from conversations overheard, from movies or television, anywhere really, so—writing down sentences or story lines or plots that occur to you throughout your day is a good first step to a finished piece.

JOURNALIST

If you write for a newspaper or magazine, you could be considered a journalist—a writer of news/nonfiction articles.

> Reporters and interviewers
> could both
> claim this title.

The word *journalist* usually refers to writers who report on current events, about people of interest, or sometimes just about the issues of the day.

Anyone writing for newspapers or even glossy magazines can be considered a journalist.

A journalist collects and disseminates information about current events, people, trends, and issues. Depending on the context, the term *journalist* also includes various types of editors and visual journalists, such as photographers, graphic artists, and page designers.

K-I-S-S THEROY

Reminding yourself to "keep it simple, stupid" is helpful when editing your own work.

Less
is often better
than more.

Although this term is not widely used by editors, it is a term that helps writers when they talk to themselves (and yes, writers are famous of this act).

When you are writing, sometimes details get too lengthy. By cutting out some of the adverbs and adjectives, it will tighten the work, making it a more powerful piece.

LAD LIT

Stories written especially for the male reader.

> Stories and Stuff
> for guys.

Writing fiction for the young adult can be as sexist as adult fiction. Although there are certainly crossovers (*Harry Potter* is one), books about a girl and her horse probably won't be of much interest to boys, and stories about motorcycles might not interest girls. This subgenre was created to further define where a book belongs in the genre jungle.

LEAD/DREK/WALK-OFF

In newspapers and magazines, an article has a lead (beginning), a drek (middle), and a walk-off (closing).

Newspaper slang
for
a written piece.

Although this newspapers slang may not be widely used in present day, some publishers do still use it.

Lead: The beginning or intro (who/what/where).

Drek: The middle where the story unfolds (how/why).

Walk-off: The ending when the story is wrapped up and finished.

LEAD TIME

The exact time to submit the piece (how long before it is to be published).

A deadline

for

a writer.

Writers, even if doing freelance work, will need to know when the piece is due. If you want to know how much time you have until the deadline, you might ask what the lead time is.

A monthly publication might have an expectation of submissions thirty days in advance, and holiday deadlines are usually longer. (For example, a six-month lead time for Christmas, Easter, or Fourth of July publications is not unusual.)

Depending on the publication and its needs, lead times will vary. Guidelines should include this information, but if it's not stated there, be sure to ask.

LIBEL

A misrepresentation of a person that causes harm.

Lies
that can come back
to haunt.

Checking your facts behind your story is *very* important. If you write and publish hearsay without really knowing the true facts, it could cause you a problem (maybe financial).

Libel is a false, malicious statement published in mainstream media (on the Internet or in a newspaper or magazine, etc.) about a person or place.

If the statements are only spoken, they are called slander (synonymous with defamation) and could also trigger a lawsuit or other unhappy results.

LIKE-BOOK COMPARISONS

Who else writes what you write?

Which books would be next to yours
in the bookstore?

Part of the business of getting published is knowing who else in the writing field writes books like you do. (Submission guidelines sometimes ask for comparison books or comparison authors.)

So this is how to figure it out. First know what genre your book fits into. Then go to a bookstore and look in that section (mystery, romance, etc.) and see the books. You will probably recognize some of the authors and now you know who else writes in that genre and who writes books that are similar to yours. You have comparison authors.

Examples:
Maeve Binchy writes contemporary fiction books about relationships and ordinary people. So does Debbie Macomber.

Stephen King writes horror, suspense, and speculative fiction. So does Dean Koontz

LIMITED EDITONS

A predetermined number of copies printed.

> Could be a lot
> or a few.

The limited edition of a book is usually restricted in the number of copies produced, although in fact the number may be very low or very high.

Coffee-table books (oversized and more picture book than literary) are usually limited in how many are published, and sometimes a reprint of an older book (like a classic) could be a limited edition.

Don't confuse this with a special edition, which implies there is extra material of some kind included. For example, a book about growing lavender may include a packet of seeds.

LINE SPACING

The number of spaces between each line of type in a manuscript.

> To double space or not?
> That is the question.

Most submission guidelines state that the manuscript should be double spaced, no additional space between paragraphs, indented paragraphs, etc. The reason for this is the readability factor. It's easier on the eyes from someone who reads a lot of things all day long. It also leaves room if an editor or agent wants to make notes.

LITERARY FICTION

Fiction that claims to hold literary merit as opposed to being of a specific genre, or popular fiction.

Will it stand
the test of time?

In very broad terms, literary fiction focuses more on style, psychological depth, and the characters in comparison to mainstream fiction, which may focus more on plot and narrative. Literary fiction could also be something that does not fit into any specific genre.

Sometimes these fiction pieces can be characterized as *lasting fiction* (literature that continues to be read and is still in-demand many decades and perhaps centuries after the author has died (Shakespeare, for example).

To understand what literary fiction is, it might help if you see what it isn't. Literary fiction is not chick lit, mystery, science fiction, or horror, although they can be good literature in themselves, and literary fiction can incorporate certain aspects of genre fiction such as building tension, good versus evil, etc. It's a fine line of separation sometimes.

MAINSTREAM FICTION

A fiction book that contains strong writing and plot that will interest many readers.

Read
by many.

Mainstream fiction can generally be described as any genre fiction that sells well. It has also been described as fiction that will have a strong plot but maybe doesn't fit into a single genre. *Gone with the Wind* might fit into this category. It had action, drama, romance, and history and certainly sold well (and still does).

Generally speaking, each genre has its own following. Stephen King readers probably won't be reading books by Debbie Macomber, and readers of John Grisham most likely will not be reading Mary Kay Andrews. Each genre and subgenre carries dedicated readers, although some may delve into other types of books. Some books are also considered crossovers (into other genres).

Each reader will find their own preference (perhaps in several genes, each written by a different author.)

MANUSCRIPT

Any written piece can be called a manuscript before and after it is published.

Handwritten
or typed.

Writers may jot their ideas down on envelopes and scraps of paper and finally get around to putting these ideas into a semblance of order. This written piece of work can be called a manuscript—something written. It could be fiction, nonfiction, or poetry; they all fall under this description.

Interchangeable terms that also describe this are your piece, your body of work, your file, or just your work.

MARGINS

The space left on the top, sides, and bottom of your manuscript.

> White area
> that's not written on.

When you are ready to submit your work for publication, most guidelines will request your manuscript have one-inch margins. This means one inch measured from the edge of the paper to the text. There are margins on the top, bottom, and right and left sides of the page.

Beginning writers might reason that there needs to be more space on the left side (leaving room for binding), but be assured that the publisher will format your work for the printing phase.

MARKETING/MARKETING PLAN

Knowing who your audience is and where your book will sell is part of a marketing plan.

Plan
to sell.

If your book is nonfiction (maybe about gardening), you'll want to be aware that to sell your book it has to be available to people who would like to read it. However, being aware is not enough—you have to make a plan to put your book into these readers' hands. If your book is fiction (perhaps blood-and-guts action), you probably won't sell too many if you put it into a women's boutique. Place your book for sale in locations where your reader frequents, and more sales will happen.

Knowing your audience is the first rule. Who will read your book?

The second thing you will need to do is establish where these people are and how to get your book into their field of vision so they can/will buy it. Also, where to advertise is important. Figuring this out will give you a marketing plan.

With this plan in place you will have a good idea where your books should be for sale, what you can do to help the sales (give talks about the subject?), and where you can do a book signing to help your book sell.

All of the above are important in a plan to get your book to the correct market/readers, (and to sell lots of books is really the master plan, right?).

MASS-MARKET BOOKS

Books that you see in bookstores, supermarkets, and airports are those that appeal to the widest market—the mass market.

> Everywhere you look
> you see these books.

Books are like any product of any industry. The more places you can locate the product for the public to see, the more you will sell. Impulse buying is a good thing in the book business.

Some authors are considered mass-market writers. Their books sell to a large audience. These are the authors everyone has heard of like J.K. Rowling and Stephen King. Their books are sold in grocery stores, malls, airports, bus terminals, and train stations. Lots of authors fall into this category, and being there is an aspiration of most beginning writers too.

MAST HEAD

In the front part of a magazine or maybe on the editorial page of a newspaper, you'll find all the business info about the publisher.

The
about me
of a publication.

In a publication such as a magazine or newspaper, the masthead usually contains all the business information about the publisher and perhaps other information, including the board of directors, advertising rates, address for submissions, business address, or how many times a year it is published. It could also include the publisher's logo.

MEMOIR
(See also Autobiography and Bio)

The true story of what a person *remembers* and what their life was like before now.

Famous

or not.

Anyone can write their own memoirs—those stories they remember about the past events of their life that will enlighten and perhaps amuse and entertain others (maybe their family).

Under the genre memoir comes autobiography (life story written by the person), biography (written about the person by someone else), and memoir (written by the person as they remember certain events/happenings.)

MIDDLE GRADE
(See also YA/Young Adult)

This is part of a subgenre of young adult fiction.

> Not little kids
> any more.

The genre of YA/young adult includes several subgenres. The main thing that differentiates a middle grade fiction novel from a young adult book is that the protagonist is ten to fourteen years old and is dealing with the problems and concerns of becoming an adolescent.

Harry Potter books are a good example, although that particular series turned out to be of interest to all generations.

MODEL RELEASE

Signed release for use of a photograph in a publication, even if it's not a picture of a model.

Get the signature
BEFORE
PUBLISHISHING.

If you want to include photos of a person or even several people in your manuscript, remember you will probably want to get a signed release from the subject(s) in the photo. If you fail to get the release, it could result in a lawsuit later (after publication).

A model release, known also as a liability waiver, is a legal release typically signed by the subject(s) of a photograph that grants permission to publish the photograph.

If in doubt about this release and the forms required, a visit to a lawyer would be a good idea.

MOM LIT
(See also Romance)

A subgenre under romance (for and about women who have children).

Mommy and me.

Mom lit stories are romantic adventures about single women (with children) who are looking for romance. The stories could also be about the adventures of being romantically entangled and dealing with the children's involvement.

MULTIFACETED

Referring to character development: people in your stories need to have multiple interests and activities to make them interesting to the reader, just like real people are multifaceted.

Referring to a story line: plots need ups and downs for the same reasons.

> Boring is not what you want
> for your characters
> or storyline.

If you give your characters emotions and situations where the reader can see their true character, or lack thereof, and if you give your plot an unexpected twist, you can have a multifaceted read.

One of the best ways to keep a reader engaged in your story is to create well rounded (although perhaps flawed) characters, ones the reader can connect with and have feelings for. Most of the time it's best to avoid stereotypes and cliché character traits (but sometimes stereotypes and clichés can work for your story).

MULTIPLE SUBMISSIONS
(See also Shotgun Submissions)

Submitting your manuscript to several publishers or agents at the same time.

The shotgun
approach.

Publishing houses and agents are not pleased when they think you have submitted your manuscript to several places at the same time (without telling them).

Here's the problem: A manuscript is received. It is sent to an in-house reader. They then send it on to the next step (maybe a supervisor), and they read it and make recommendations and send it on—but wait—here comes a letter from the author saying the manuscript was accepted by another office. The publisher then feels all of its effort and time was wasted for no results.

For the writer, it is frustrating to send out a manuscript and wait two or three months for a reply only to have to send it out again. If a multiple-submission (shotgun) approach is decided upon, it is only right to state up front that it is a simultaneous submission (perhaps at the bottom of the query letter). Then the recipient can decide if they want to invest its time.

MYSTERIES
(See also Genre)

Stories that can contain suspense, offer a conflict, and then offer clues for a successful conclusion.

> Did you see
> what happened?

A story that gives the reader a crime or incident and then shows clues along the way so that a conclusion is reached and the puzzle is solved is considered a mystery. Of course, there are many types (subgenres) of mysteries. See the Mystery heading under *Genre* for a detailed list of subgenres.

MYTHS
(See also Folklore and Speculative Fiction)

Stories originating in traditions and used to explain life and circumstances.

Lessons
from stories.

From the Greek word *mythos*, it means *story* or *word*.

Myths are defined as tales believed as true, usually sacred, set in the distant past or other worlds, or parts of this world.

The characters in myths may contain superhuman traits like Hercules (extra physical strength) and extra special skills like Mars (the Roman god of war).

There are also many modern-day mythical stories still being written. This genre is far from dead.

NARRATIVE NONFICTION

True stories and facts presented in story form.

Nicely
put facts.

Memoirs and some how-to books can be called narrative nonfiction—stories told by a narrator though their point of view.

These facts and information, written in story form pieces, have a beginning, middle, and end, as in all stories.

NETWORKING

Meeting and getting to know other people in the writing field.

It really is
who you know.

In the writing world, knowing people in high places is definitely a good thing. Writers' conferences are a great place to meet and get to know other writers, publishers, and agents. You may also meet people who can teach you to write better, or could professionally edit your finished work, or maybe simply help you keep going in this tough business.

NEW EYES

Someone other than the author reading a piece.

A new look
at these words.

Many writers can benefit from someone else reading their work. This person can look at the formatting, punctuation, and story line with a fresh pair of eyes—new eyes.

When a writer reads his own work, it's very easy to fill in words (that aren't there), or overlook changes in point of view. Reading your manuscript out loud helps, but soliciting a new pair of eyes to give your piece the once-over is never a mistake.

NEWSLETTER (FOR WRITERS)

A regularly distributed publication (on-line), usually for an especially designated group.

News
for the
writing world.

There are many on-line newsletters for writers. A subscription (usually free) can be obtained to address almost any topic. Want to find an agent? Looking for a writers' conference? Want to join a critique group? Interested in contests? There is a newsletter for each of these interests.

Almost all writing magazines and writers organizations have on-line newsletters. These are treasure troves of information. Consider signing up for one or two.

A couple of on-line newsletters for you to subscribe to:
Writersdigest.com
SCBWI.com (Society of Children's Book Writers and
Illustrators)
Glimmertrain.com (for contests)

NICHE MARKET

A narrow place (marketplace/reader interest) where your book fits.

A very special
topic.

Some books have topics or themes that put them into a very narrow, focused (niche) market. If a book is written about caring for pets, that could be of interest to a broad group of people, but if the book is only about caring for parrots, then that is a special niche book because probably a much smaller and specialized group would be interested.

NOIR FICTION

Dark fiction and certainly black humor.

> Some people think the darker,
> the better.

Noir is a special kind of fiction (and film) that was made especially during the 1940s and 1950s. It's a negative, cynical view of life, often focusing on crime and vice in cities. Not happy or lite stories, these are about the ugly/savage/dark parts of living.

NONFICTION

Any story that is true.

                    Truth in telling.

   Stories such as memoirs, how-to books, and perhaps travel
or other adventures that are told using the facts of the story
with no embellishments is called nonfiction. All true stories, no
made-up parts.

NOVEL
(See also Novella and Genre)

A long, fictional story involving a plot (and perhaps several subplots).

Reading

for

entertainment.

A novel is a book containing a long, narrative story written in literary prose. It can belong to more than one genre, and is usually at least sixty thousand words in length.

Novels are considered fiction. A nonfiction book of the same length (even if written in story form) is *not* called a novel.

NOVELLA

All the aspects of a novel but shorter.

Smaller
than a novel.

A novella is just a very short novel with fewer conflicts than its big brother, but it is more complicated than a short story. The true novella can have endings that are not truly resolved, and a novella typically does not have chapters, only using white space to divide happenings and scene changes. It's more like a long, long short story than a short novel.

NUGGETS
(See also Snippets)

Very, very short informational or entertaining pieces.

Brief

happenings.

Readers Digest and *Taste of Home* are magazines that have little nuggets of information at the bottom or sides of their pages.

Some are jokes, some are entertaining stories, and some add information to the accompanying article.

ON-LINE

A slang term that means connected to the Internet.

Plugged into the
World Wide Web.

Being on-line could include chatting, playing games, or checking facts for your manuscript.

The computer can be a wonderful help and tool for writers, especially with the resources available on the Internet.

There are many websites of interest to writers—places that answer questions when you are doing research (**ask.com** or **wickipedia.com**), or they can offer help finding market listings for your piece (**writersmarket.com**).

Writers can also set up appointments for interviews (using e-mail chat), or perhaps you could find places where you could submit your work to be published on-line (e-publishing). There is a whole world of possibilities on the Internet.

ONE-DIMENSIONAL

Showing only one side of a situation or character.

Very few people or activities
are only one-sided.

Dimensional means the depth, length, and height of something. If you have characters that are only one-dimensional (no sense of humor, no apparent feelings about anything), it could be less interesting than if you let the reader see the substance of that person. Show what makes the character laugh or cry, or what they would do in a given situation.

Readers want to know all about each of the characters, especially if it's a bad guy. They want to know what makes the characters tick.

ONE-ON-ONE

Meeting with an editor or an agent—just the two of you.

Time to memorize
your elevator speech.

During writers' conferences, the opportunity might be available for you to meet an editor or an agent face-to-face—just the two of you in a discussion about your writing in a one-on-one chat.

If you have done your homework and you already know that the agent or editor is interested in your type of writing, then you have a perfect opportunity to sell yourself and your writing.

If the person asks you to send your manuscript to them, be sure to ask if you should mark the envelope "requested material" or just address it to his/her attention. Then when you send it in, remember you should still mark the outside of the envelope with the name of the conference, and of course you will address it directly to the person you talked to (making sure the name is spelled correctly). This marking on the envelope with the conference name will show the office receiver that this was requested material (when you met at the conference where you were invited to submit), and the enclosed manuscript isn't something for the slush pile.

OPENING LINE
(See also Hook)

The first sentence of a piece.

> Oh, so important.

In order to attract a reader to the rest of the story, an opening line is important and might be the most important line in the whole piece.

Many buyers of books read the first line to see if they might like reading the rest of the story. If they like that, they might go on to read the first paragraph. If that makes them want to read more, then they are hooked. So you can see how well-crafted the first line and paragraph must be.

OUTLINE

A general summary of ideas for a story.

Sometimes
a good first step
in writing.

There are many ways to start writing a piece, and one is to write an outline.

You set down the major point of your book, fill in a few sub-points, and you have the start of an outline.

Most of us learned to outline in school, and for a writer, this can be a good tool. Some writers even list the names of the characters and what they're doing in the story:

Example:
I. Joe
    A.   Seventeen years old
    B.   Captain of high school football team
    C.   Never had a date

II. Sheila
    A.   Thirty-five years old
    B.   New teacher in school
    C.   Goes to high school football games
    D.   Invites Joe to her home for tutoring

III. Joe's Father Jim
    A.   Notices Sheila's interest in Joe
    B.   Doesn't like the situation
    C.   Threatens Sheila

IV. Sheila goes to Joe's house
    A.   Jim and Sheila get friendly

V. Joe comes home unexpectedly

VI. Joe runs away to a Buddhist monastery

Write lots of dialogue and inter-action between the characters, and you have a story.

OVER-THE-TRANSOM
(See also Unsolicited Manuscripts and Slush Pile)

The stacks of unsolicited manuscripts at a publisher's or agent's office.

> If they're not requested,
> they may only sit and wait.

Over-the-transom is a slang term used in the publishing world that refers to unsolicited manuscripts that have arrived in an editors or agent's office. There was no invitation to send the full manuscript.

This phrase came to be when someone stated that writers had just as much chance of getting published by sending unsolicited manuscripts as they would if they just threw the manuscript over the transom into the office (of an agent or publisher).

OVER-VIEW

A very short synopsis of your piece.

Just a few
sentences.

This is a review of your piece that is shorter than a synopsis or blurb—just one or two sentences at most.

Example:
This is a story of five generations of women who all marry murderers, but none of them know it.

PAGE NUMBERS

Located either on the bottom of each page or in the upper-right corner.

Just to keep track.

All manuscripts should contain page numbers. This should become an automatic action for writers so pages can be kept in order. Page numbers should either be located in the header or footer.

Think of this: You labor over a manuscript, and it is finally in the condition ready for submitting. You send it in to that special place that is just right for your genre, but when it's taken out of the envelope, it drops, and the pages scatter. It's not a problem to reassemble if the pages are numbered, but what if they're not? *Oops* does not cover the problem.

PAPERBACK BOOK
(See also Softcover Books and Trade Paperback Books)

Any published book that does not have a hardcover.

> Light and handy
> to carry.

It is not uncommon for a book to be published first as a hardcover book (one with a thick, stiff cardboard covers) and then later as a softcover or paperback book.

Many of these paperback books are mass-market reads sold not only in bookstores but grocery stores, drug stores, airports, train and bus stations, and anywhere else the reading public might be.

PARAGRAPHS

Groups of sentences all relating to the same point.

A bunch of sentences
that are
indented at the beginning.

Paragraphs can be written in block style (no indent) or with the first sentence indented five spaces if you're using a typewriter or indented a tab space on the computer. The indented way is the preferred method when submitting a double-spaced manuscript or piece. It is easier to read, and making it easier for an agent or publisher to read is always a good thing.

It's also important to note that dialogue is shown with each speaker starting his own paragraph when it's their turn to speak, and the spoken words are set off by quotation marks ("..").

Also, try not to start every paragraph with the same word. It becomes monotonous (unless you're using this tactic for emphasis).

PARTS OF A STORY

The three parts of a story are the beginning (hook), middle (conflict), and end (resolution.)

Very much like life.

All stories should start with a sentence (and paragraph) that will make the reader want to read more—the hook.

And all stories should have a conflict, even if it's as minor as finding a lost sock. This is the middle, or conflict.

Now all that's left to write is the ending, which is the resolution to the conflict.

That's an easy formula to follow, right?

PEN NAME
(See also Pseudonym)

The name a writer uses instead of their own.

Who to be

or

not to be.

Some authors prefer to sign their work with a name other than their own when they write. It's called a pen name, pseudonym, and a *nom de plume*.

Reasons for using a pen name vary. In the early eighteen hundreds, women who wrote novels adopted men's names, because it was thought to be un-ladylike to be a writer. Even now, some women who write books read mostly by men (like blood-and-gut thrillers); often use pen names or pseudonyms, and some men who write romance novels use a female pen name.

Remember, using a pen name can be useful if you don't want the reader to know who you are, but beware—doing book signings could be tricky.

PIECE OF WORK
(See also Manuscript)

What you wrote—your poem, short story, novel, etc. Your written work is your piece of work.

> The words piece
> and
> manuscript
> can be used interchangeably.

Your written work is sometimes referred to as your piece of work. This could be any writing before it is submitted for publication.

A manuscript (no matter how long or in what genre) is the name publishers' use for submissions, (but some could refer to it as your piece, or piece of work).

PITCH
(See also Elevator Speech)

What you say to interest a prospective publisher or agent about your piece.

A
selling speech.

Giving a pitch is just telling a prospective publisher or agent about your story and making it so interesting that they will ask questions and then ask to see the complete manuscript.

Many writers' conferences hold workshops so you can practice your pitch. These how-to-pitch workshops are worth going to. They can give you hints and tips that you might not have thought about so you can make yours the perfect pitch (sales job).

PITCH SLAM

A group of writers, all pitching their stories to several agents and publishers.

Of course,
they're not all talking at once.

A pitch slam is a session where writers take turns at a microphone to pitch their stories to editors seated as an audience. Usually a writer gets sixty seconds. Here's a statement taken from a recap on the Internet about a recent conference where a slam pitch session was held:

> "More than 15 eager writers queued up to the microphones to pitch their stories, each allotted 60 seconds to hook an editor or agent. In return, the editors offered constructive feedback for each idea. By the end of the session, more than one pitch seemed to have found a home.
>
> Tightly packaged, colorful pitches with compelling characters scored high points. Some writers struggled to pitch stories, not topics. Others failed to underscore a story's novelty or tried to pack multiple stories into one. The editors advised writers to find the new angle on a story, or told them to emphasize the conflict, or present counterintuitive ideas in their pitches."

PLAGIARISM
(See also Libel)

The wrongful act of a writer using another's writing and representing it as their own.

Lying
to the Nth degree.

Using words written by another writer can be done easily enough by giving credit to the creator of those words, but using someone else's words without permission or without giving the credit due, is stealing. If you do this, **beware:** Lawsuits could follow.

PLATFORM
(See also Credentials)

Your writing credentials. Why *you* are qualified to write a particular piece.

> Why me?
> Here's why.

Sometimes an agent or publisher will ask a writer to explain his platform. What they want to know is what makes you the person to write about this topic.

Writers of nonfiction run into this often. Fiction writers may also be asked about credentials if they are writing about specific subjects, such as medical mysteries, or perhaps if their stories are situated in certain, foreign settings, such as Tibet.

A platform can be what schooling or travels you've had to give you this knowledge, what jobs you've held, or maybe just one exciting experience (like falling off a cliff in Tibet).

PLOT AND PLOT DEVELOPMENT

The plot is the main storyline of a piece of writing. It has a beginning, middle, and end.

It's what's happening.

Fiction stories have plots. The plot is the reason for, or the point of, the story. It's what happens when the characters interact.

Plot development happens when the writer starts introducing people and actions, and it doesn't finish developing until you see the end.

There are many good exercises and books written about how to develop a plot, and going to workshops at writers' conferences is another way to learn (and you can get answers to you questions). Look in magazines such as *Writer's Digest* or *The Writer* to see where a writers' conference may be taking place near you.

PLOTLINE

A very short synopsis that is generally only one sentence.

Quick explanation.

Telling about the plot of your piece to someone, like an agent or editor, is easy until they ask for just the plotline. What they want is a *very* short overview of the story. Make this a one-or-two sentence statement as intriguing as possible so that they will want more details.

Example:
A young couple gets married and then she finds out she is wife number four.

POD (PRINT ON DEMAND)

A publishing term meant to describe some types of the small press printing practices, or sometimes this describes self-publishing.

One small batch at a time.

Some small presses only print the number of books that is expected to sell. This could be a batch as small as one hundred books, and then they only print books as they are *actually ordered*—print on demand.

Self-publishing can also work this way even if the press/ publisher is larger. This practice should be spelled out in the contract for the writer to see.

POETIC LICENSE
(See also Anachronisms)

A deviation from facts to achieve a particular effect.

> Breaking the rules
> and
> maybe obscuring the facts.

Writers use poetic license when they change parts of well-known facts so that a story, plotline, or character can say or do special things. Anachronisms can also be considered poetic license. It could be a deviation of a historical fact to obtain a special effect.

Example:
When an artist paints trees blue (in a forest of green trees), he is taking poetic or artistic license.

In poetry writing, bending the rules of grammar is allowable so that the author might obtain the desired effect, sometimes to have something rhyme, or to conform to meter requirements. This is another sort of poetic license.

POETRY

Rhyming or lyric or in prose form, poetry is the art of rhythmical composition, written or spoken.

To rhyme
or not to rhyme . . .

The definition of poetry is difficult to state, and it should also be noted that there are almost as many types of poems as there are genres for prose.

Some types of poetry are:
Acrostic, where the first letter of each line forms a word,
Blank verse which is written in iambic pentameter,
Free verse which can rhyme or not and has no set metered pattern.

Here are some quotes about what some notable people think poetry is. It might help with understanding this writing form:

"The best poems say with words that which can't be said with words." (Pacific Northwest poet Rob Jacques, in his online review of Mary Oliver's *New and Selected Poems, Volume One*)

"Poetry is language at its most distilled and most powerful." (Rita Dove)

"A poem begins in delight and ends in wisdom." (Robert Frost)

"Poetry is thoughts that breathe, and words that burn." Thomas Gray (of "Gray's Elegy" fame)

"No one was ever yet a great poet, without at the same time a profound philosopher."

"Poetry is the best words in the best order." (Samuel Taylor Coleridge)

"For all good poetry is the spontaneous overflow of powerful feelings . . ." (William Wordsworth, in his Preface to *Lyrical Ballads*)

POINT OF VIEW

Who is telling the story, a narrator or a character?

Who's
doing the honors?

Someone will be telling your story. The reader will hear it through the voice of someone *in* the story or perhaps through a narrator who sees everything. This general manner of viewing situations and the attitudes is called a point of view (POV).

Following are the general points of view from which a story can be told:

First person is a narrative done by one of the characters (usually the protagonist). It is the "I" style and gives the reader only one point of view—the storyteller's as he lives it or recalls it. This person can't give you the other characters' feelings or thoughts but can only relay what they see and hear. This can be hard to sustain when a writer needs to present reasons for a given action or reactions in order to move the story line on to a conclusion.

Second person is the "you" point of view and is often too confusing. It is rarely used.

Third person is a literary style that uses "he" and "she," and the narration is not done by one of the characters but an overseer. Here, we have two choices:

Omniscient third person means there is a narrator who is all seeing. He knows what others are thinking, what happened in the past, and what's going to happen in the future, and he shares it with the reader.

<u>Limited third person</u> is when a character from the story is acting as the teller; either the protagonist or the antagonist can have this job.

Traditionally, the only time you would change a POV is at the introduction of a new character or scene, or at the start of a new chapter.

PREAMBLE

An introductory statement, (especially in legal documents).

Just a phrase
to get the story started.

A preamble is an introductory statement—a preliminary explanation. The term is particularly applied to the opening paragraph(s) of a statute of law, which can recite historical facts that may be pertinent to the issue. In other writings it may be an explanation for the way the story being discussed is written.

Example:
Although this is really an excuse for the presentation, it could nonetheless be a preamble to a writing proposal:

> "Despite what you might think after reading my work, I have taken journalism classes. I know about leads and the inverted pyramid. I just happened to fall upon writing opportunities that required me to watch lots of TV and movies and play video games. So please forgive me if my samples are lacking in the "journalistic tradition."

PREDITIONS
(See also Flashbacks)

The story moves forward, out of the time line, to explain what is expected to happen.

> Planning for the future
> is a kind of prediction.

Predictions can help explain present actions because of what is expected to happen further along in the story. These should be used carefully and sparingly, except in sci-fi, which sometimes uses prediction as a current time line.

PREFACE
(See also Foreword)

A brief introduction written by the author.

> Authors can explain
> Things.

There are many short pieces of writing that can be before the main text in a published book. They can be a preface, a foreword, a prologue, or an introduction. The preface is usually written by the author and sometimes contains a bit of history about the subject or about writing this book in particular.

Don't confuse a preface (which is written by the author) with the foreword (which is written by someone else who may give a little more background and maybe some praise).

PRE-READER
(See also Children's Books)

Read-to-me books with lots of pictures for the early reading experience.

> Reading to a child
> is a special time for everyone.

Pre-reader books, by definition, are books for the age group from birth to four years old. These books have illustrations that play a significant part in the story, and words are sparse. Generally these books are no more than thirty-two pages long but can be even less as seen below:

<u>Baby Books</u> (Ages birth to two): These books can be lullabies, nursery rhymes, repetitive words, finger playing ("Itsy Bitsy Spider"), or wordless books. The length and format varies with the content, however word count will probably be around seventy-five.

<u>Toddler Books</u> (Ages one to four): These books are generally very simple stories but they still contain a beginning, middle, and end. They should be less than three hundred words and familiar to a child's everyday life. It can be a concept book (teaching colors, numbers, shapes, etc.), or a familiar story such as *The Little Engine That Could.* They are short (twelve pages is average), and the format can be a board book (sturdy paper over a very stiff/cardboard construction), pop-ups, lift-the-flaps, or novelty books (books that make sounds or have different textures, etc.) The *Max* series of board books by Rosemary Wells or the *If You Give a Mouse a Cookie* books written by Laura Joffe Numeroff are good examples. Rhyme and repetition are popular and are enjoyable to both adults and child. And perhaps the adult will see that after only one or two readings, the child will be "reading" to the adult (from memory of course).

It's important not to forget that nonfiction picture books can be of interest up to age ten or twelve (or older). They can be the usual forty-eight pages in length or much longer depending on the subject matter, and some go up to two thousand words of text. Science and botanical books fall into this category.

It's very difficult to put a *reading group age* on any child. Children progress at their own speed and reading picture books at an early age starts a child's interest in reading that will hopefully last a lifetime.

PRESENTER

A person leading a workshop or seminar or someone in a selling position.

Teacher

or

Instructor.

Leaders of any kind of instructional situation or speakers in a classroom atmosphere can be called presenters. They present certain facts and ideas to those in the audience or class.

When a writer is selling their book and does a reading, they could also be called a presenter. They are presenting their book to readers and potential buyers.

PRETEEN
(See also Tween Books)

An early teenage group designation in the children's books genre.

> A child not ready for young adult topics
> but wants more than middle-grade subjects.

The genre designated as children's has several subgenres included in its boundaries. Tween, or preteen, is one of these subgenres.

Some children, before they are teenagers (10-13), and after they have been reading chapter books and middle-grade books, like to read about more grown-up subjects. These books are also referred to as tween books—between being a child and a teenager.

PRINT ON DEMAND
(See also POD)

Publishers that print books as they are ordered.

> Maybe just A few
> at a time.

Some publishes and small presses run/print a limited amount of books—just what they think will sell. As the orders slow down perceptively, they print only the orders they receive.

PROEM
(See also Preface or Prelude)

A brief introduction or prelude to a book.

A beginning
comment.

This is an introduction that is sometimes about the author rather than the story that has been written in the book. This word is not widely used for a preface, prelude, or introduction, but it is used especially in Old English writings and the translation loosely means "beginnings."

PROJECT

Whichever writing you are involved in at the time is considered a (your) project.

> Writing is a project
> as much as painting a wall.

A project is an all-encompassing word that you can use when you tell someone you are writing. You could say, "I have a children's book project I'm working on" or "My most recent project has sold."

PROLOGUE
(See also Foreword)

A few sentences or as much as several pages at the beginning of a piece to help set up the story line.

Information to help
readers enjoy the story.

The history or background of someone in the story, or the geography regarding the setting of the story, or maybe about the mores of a particular time period can be helpful for a reader to know.

Use a prologue much like a foreword to help enhance the reader's knowledge.

PROOFREAD

Reading a manuscript to make sure there are no mistakes in grammar, spelling, continuity of story line, or style.

Looking for fixes
is the name of this game.

Although every writer should learn how to proofread his own manuscript before it is submitted to an agent or publisher, a professional editor is probably a good investment too.

As writers everywhere know, when you read your own work, you know what it's supposed to say. Because of this, you might miss a transposition of letters or a tense that doesn't match in subject and verb. Nothing says unprofessional writer more than misspelled words or bad grammar.

One trick to help find problems is to read your work out loud in front of a mirror, because it feels like you are reading to an audience. If you stumble while reading, take note, because a fix may be needed.

PROPOSAL
(See also Book Proposal)

Book and magazine proposals are somewhat different.

> Much like proposing a marriage
> between
> a publisher and writer.

Book proposals and magazine proposals differ, and writing them is an art that takes some investigation and practice.

A nonfiction book proposal is simply telling a publisher who you are (short bio), what you have written or want to write, what you've published before (clips if you have them), why you're the right person to write a particular book (platform), how you can help sell the book (marketing plan), and what you see as competitive books (comparisons). This, along with a few chapters of your book, is pretty much what is needed. More specific information is available under the entry for "book proposal."

Magazine proposals can usually be done by e-mail or regular snail mail but differ in that you will need to send clips, a one-page synopsis of what you propose to write, and a detailed bio reflecting your credentials/platform for the proposed writing project. Most magazines will offer guidelines with phone numbers and e-mail addresses, so you can contact the correct person. E-mail is fast becoming the way query letters are sent. As always, follow the guidelines given.

If you're looking for detailed help in putting together a proposal, look at these:

How to Write a Nonfiction Book Proposal by Stephan Blake Mettee for nonfiction writing

And

Write the Perfect Book Proposal: 10 that Sold and Why by Jeff Herman and Deborah Levine Herman for fiction writing.

PROTAGONIST

The principal character in a work of fiction.

This is probably your hero
but not necessarily.

The main or principal character in your piece is the protagonist. He/she is usually the good guy but not always. A murderer could be the main character, or even a talking pig as in *Babe*.

PSEUDONYM
(See also Pen Name)

An author writing under an assumed name (one not his own) can be said to be writing under a pseudonym (or perhaps a pen name.)

> An author by any other name
> is still the same.

There are many reasons for an author to not want to use their given name on a book. A professor at a college may want to write steamy romance novels and not want anyone to know. A person may write true crime and not want to give any associated criminals a way to find him. Another reason for using a made-up name is when a writer is very prolific, and the publisher or agents might not want to saturate the market. Stephen King is one of those authors who has written under more than one name.

PUBLIC DOMAIN

After a period of time, a copyright runs its course. The material then belongs to the public and can be reproduced without compensation to anyone.

Free and clear
to copy.

If a manuscript or story was published before 1882, it is in the public domain, but credit should be given to the author if you use even just an excerpt.

Likewise, if a song was published before 1922, it is in the public domain. Parts or the whole song can be used in a story (but any lyrics used should be accredited to the composer.)

Checking to see if a published piece is in the public domain is complicated, but there are law firms that specialize in doing just that.

PUBLISHED

Your hard copy writings printed and distributed, or posted on the Internet for public consumption. It could be in a newsletter, newspaper, magazine, book, e-zine, or in any other form.

> Write, write;
> submit, submit;
> and then get published . . . hopefully.

Being published means your writing is printed and distributed so others can read it. Even writing your self-published newsletters to the family or for the members of your church qualifies you as *being published*. Don't forget that e-publishing also counts.

PUBLISHER
(CONVENTIONAL AND SUBSIDY)

A company that prints your book and may help to distribute it for sale.

Your work printed
for
consumption.

Conventional publishers sign a contract with an author for the right to publish their book. The publisher will edit, design the cover, and print the book. Next comes marketing and distributing the book. Profits to the author (the royalties) are based on book sales.

Subsidy publishers charge the author for typesetting and printing the book but market the book at their expense. The publisher and author share profits by the method set out in a contract. This kind of publishing comes close to vanity press publishing or self-publishing and should be looked at closely before the author signs anything or spends money.

Print-on-demand books can be subsidy publishers too, but they might do little advertising or marketing and may only print the books as they sell, as opposed to printing books in advance of sales.

Vanity press is another word for self-publishing. The author takes care of all phases of the publishing (and pays for it), is responsible for all sales, and keeps all of the profits.

PUNCH LINE

This could be a surprise point in the story or a surprise ending.

> The strong point
> of a funny story.

In a joke, the punch line would be the point of the joke. In a story, it's the point of the story.

This phrase usually describes a humorous piece.

PURPLE PROSE

Very ornate language used in descriptions of people, places, and things.

Can you
picture it?

Writings full of flowery, descriptive language can be referred to as purple prose. Taking the time to set up an object or place and then describing it beautifully down to the last detail is considered purple prose. Many readers will love these wonderful word pictures.

A mistake is sometimes made if you mix up blue prose with purple prose. Blue prose (in bygone days) referred to naughty words or deeds in a story.

QUERY
(See also Book Proposal and Proposal)

Letters to a prospective publisher that provides information about you (the writer), and an idea of what you'd like published (a sort of pre-proposal letter).

> If you're given guidelines
> for a query letter . . .
> follow them closely.

So you've written your piece, it's polished and perfect in grammar and punctuation, and now you want someone to publish it. However, first you need to find the proper place to send it, so you look in *Writer's Guide,* go to bookstores and see who publishes like books, read about publishers in magazines, or find an agent you think would be a good fit. Next you need to send a letter to see if a particular book publisher, magazine editor, or agent is actually interested in seeing your work. That's where a query letter comes into play.

Publishers will usually spell out in their guidelines what they want to see in a query letter, but if they don't, here are some suggestions:

Nonfiction:

In this letter, include all your contact information (including your website if you have one), your credentials for writing the nonfiction book in question, the reason you think it will fit into their publishing scheme (for example, the book is about trout fishing, and they publish books about outdoor recreation and have books about fishing on their published list), and a short synopsis of what the piece is about.

Don't confuse the query letter with a proposal package. Usually a proposal is sent only when a publisher invites you to do so. You will have already sent the query letter. When you receive a reply requesting a proposal, you will follow the guidelines exactly. If guidelines aren't available, find a good book on proposals and follow those directions.

Fiction:
Include all your contact information, a synopsis (including like books or authors), a short paragraph about yourself, and perhaps why you're sending the query letter to this agent/editor.

Again, follow any guidelines set forth.

QUIRKY FICTION

Not a specific genre; something outside of those categories where the majority of writing fits.

Being different
isn't always bad.

Not fitting into a genre makes a manuscript a little harder to classify, and *quirky* is one of the names some editors use for any writing that falls outside the box.

If you write a piece about ladies' bridge clubs and what the ladies really talk about, it might be hard to tell what genre it belongs to.

A simple test is to answer these questions: Is this a romance? Is this about history? Is this a mystery? Is this a memoir? Continue this process through the list of general genres. If none fit, it might be quirky—just something a little different.

Looking for books in the library or at the bookstores that are about similar topics will help you know which publishers might be interested even if it is quirky fiction.

QUOTE

Including in your writing what someone already said/wrote.

Words
from
someone else.

A spoken statement from a person or writings of an authority on your subject can help to make your nonfiction piece stronger and will add credibility to your work.

If you use a quote in your manuscript, it should be set apart with quotation marks or, if it is a long quote, it can be set off in as a block quote using an extra half inch margin on both sides, and no quote marks. And don't forget to identify the person you are quoting.

READER/EDITOR
(See also Audience)

In a publishing office there are readers of manuscripts. Some are also called editors.

> All the people who read your writing,
> both before publishing and after.

Publishing houses employ people to read the manuscripts they receive. In some offices, they are called editors; however, they are *not* to be confused with those people called editors who proofread, make corrections, and give editorial remarks about your manuscript and help make your piece better.

The word readers also means the people you think would like to read your work—your audience.

READINGS

Authors reading their own work to the public.

> "Now here's the author to read to you from
> their latest book."
> Those are beautiful words to a writer.

Part of all marketing plans should be for the author to do public readings from their book. These readings can be held in schools, libraries, bookstores, or by invitation to groups.

A writer should prepare for this day by practicing. Try reading out loud in front of a mirror (don't forget to look up sometimes). This not only gives you practice hearing yourself read but will help give you confidence. Also, if public appearances are not your favorite part of the writing/publishing process, just remember that for each reading you give, you will sell books. That should give the author incentive.

REDLINE
(See also Blueline)

Red ink could be used for making editing marks.

Red pencils
have long been a tool of editing.

Redlining on a part of a manuscript usually means "this needs work." It could also mean "delete this part." When in doubt, ask your editor.

REJECTION LETTER

A letter from an agent or publisher stating they will not be publishing your piece at this time.

> If you never submit,
> you won't get rejections,
> but you won't get published either.

Rejection letters are not the easy part of submitting your writing. The first one you get will probably hurt your feelings, but you need to learn early on that in the publishing business, rejection letters are *never* personal. Don't let a piece of paper make you decide you're wasting your time as a writer or that the world hates you. This letter only means that particular publisher's reader or editor did not think the manuscript was a fit for them—at this time.

If they send a note of encouragement with your rejection letter (For example, "If this story contained more action, we would be interested in taking another look."), *pay attention.* This is a good rejection letter with a comment. The publisher said it would look at it again, so decide to rewrite and resubmit using the suggestions. Remember to address your resubmission to the person who signed the letter.

Don't give up. Letters of rejection don't mean you're a bad writer. They just mean the piece in question wasn't what that agent/publisher wanted to publish on the day they read it, or . . . it might mean you didn't do your homework to find a correct fit.

REPRESENTATIVE/LAWYER
(See also Agents)

People and agencies who know the publishing world and can help you in your publishing quest.

People who can represent
you
and your writing.

At some point in your writing career, you might find you need to be represented by either an agent, who talks to publishers on your behalf, or by a lawyer, who can help with contracts or legal discussions. Neither is a necessity, but they both can be useful.

Agents help a writer get published by offering his manuscript(s) to publishers. Publishers often prefer to receive manuscripts in this fashion rather than the over-the-transom manuscripts, as the saying goes.

When you receive a contract from a publisher or agent, it's a good idea to have a lawyer who's familiar with the publishing world review it before you sign. It makes good sense to protect yourself in this fashion.

REQUESTED MATERIAL

A notation you put on the outside of an envelope or manuscript box when sending a manuscript to a publisher that has indeed requested it.

> Make sure your manuscript
> really
> has been requested
> before you use this phrase.

It's possible that after hearing your pitch, an agent or editor may comment that it sounds interesting and suggest that you send in a query. Don't mistake this for anything other than what it is. It simply means his office handles stories such as you described, and a query letter should be sent in for consideration.

If you send your query letter to a publisher or agent and receive a reply that requests a proposal or the manuscript, *then* you should write "requested material" on the box or envelope. Usually the requester (the publisher or agent) will tell you to mark the outside of the envelope with this phrase; however, **only do this** if you are actually asked to do so.

Do not take this method as a shortcut to getting quicker attention for your manuscript!

If your manuscript is submitted with this marking without an invitation, you will be shooting yourself in the foot. Not only will the publisher not look at what was sent, but they may *never* look at any of your future your submissions.

And remember, editors talk to each other, and so do agents. Don't be foolish! Follow the rules.

RESEARCH

Using history or reference books, or looking on the Internet to check facts for your story is called research.

Seeking truths.

Checking the facts for any nonfiction piece is a necessity. Information gleaned from resources such as library archives, reference books at universities, or the Internet can make you much more informed of details.

A good practice is to make note of where you find your facts (perhaps listing them on index cards, including publication name and page numbers), and save them. Documenting your work at a later date will be much easier if you have this information at your fingertips.

RESOLVE/RESOLUTION

Ending issues you have introduced into the story.

> Revealing the murderer
> is resolving a conflict.

In every good story there is a plot. Most plots have conflicts of some kind. Revealing the solution to this conflict, or resolving the conflict, is what resolution means. Letting the reader know the resolution is a plot enhancer, or maybe even the point of the story.

Unresolved situations could make for an unhappy reader, and an unhappy reader will not look for other books by the same author. If a writer plans to end the book so the reader wants to read a sequel, they need to weigh the risk of leaving any major situation hanging up in the air—unresolved.

RESUME
(See also Author Biography/Bio)

Information about your education and working life.

> Wait—
> this probably doesn't represent
> your writing credentials.

The résumé of an author should not be confused with his writing bio/biography. Traditionally, a résumé shows your work history and educational records, while a biography shows your experience (and perhaps germane education), that makes you the correct person to write the proposed manuscript or piece.

Résumés generally show education and career/workplaces, but not necessarily writing experience.

RETURN POSTAGE
(See also IRC and SASE/SAE/SAP)

Postage sent on an envelope so that you can receive a reply from the publisher or agent about your submission.

Make sure the return envelope
Contains adequate postage.

When you submit your manuscript, most guidelines tell you to also send a SASE (self-addressed stamped envelope) so they may send you a reply. Sometimes this reply will be a request for you to send more information (perhaps request a proposal), sometimes they will ask for the complete manuscript, and sometimes they will use it so they can return your submission (hopefully with comments).

When sending your manuscript or piece anywhere outside of the United States postal system, an IRC (international reply coupon) needs to be included. You purchase this in your local U.S. Post Office. Leave it loose, not glued, as it needs to be taken to the post office of that foreign country and converted to whatever is required to put postage on the package for its return.

REVISING
(See also Editing)

Changing your written words; making corrections in usage and punctuation or even rewriting.

> Revising is editing,
> and
> editing is revising.

Revising and editing happens in several ways. Some writers revise (fix, change, and edit) only after they have written the total piece, some try to write the piece perfectly the first time, and some create several pages and then go back and edit.

Another way to edit so you can revise is when you finish writing a passage, a scene, or a chapter, read it out loud. This lets your ear hear what your reader will read and what you have written. It helps you pick up on incorrect grammar and phrasing.

There is no right or wrong way to revise and/or edit. Each writer must find the way that works best for them.

RHETORICAL

Rhetorical comes from the word *rhetoric*, which means the art of communicating.

Rhetorical question:
Isn't it obvious?

The word *rhetorical* is a form of *rhetoric*.

Rhetorical modes of speech or writing are a big phrase that simply means giving facts to the audience (in this case the reader).

There are four common modes:

Exposition: The purpose of exposition is to provide background and inform the readers about the plot, characters, setting, and theme of a story.

Argumentation: This usually means debate (probably between characters).

Descriptive: Primarily used to tell the reader what people look like and about settings.

Narrative: The narrator tells the story with very little character chitchat.

Seldom do you hear the term *rhetorical mode* used, but if you do, you'll have a start at understanding what is meant.

RIGHTS
(See also Copyright)

This is a publishing term; First North American Rights, All Rights, First Time Rights, Subsidy Rights, etc. are part of a contract between a writer and publisher regarding ownership of a writer's work.

> It's time to get a lawyer involved
> when they start talking about
> who owns the rights.

Contracts from publishers spell out who will have the rights of ownership for the piece you have written. Remember that as soon as it is written, the copyright belongs to you; however, when you sign a contract, you are assigning the rights to someone else, and that is a legal action. Before you sign a contract, it might be sensible to have an attorney familiar with the writing world go over the contract with you so you understand *exactly* what you are signing away.

It's important to remember that a lawyer can help, but as a writer, you need to understand this list of rights:

All Rights: everything listed on the contract, and anything else a publisher thinks up.

Electronic Rights: printing or displaying your piece as it refers to computer technology (print on demand, e-books, CDs, etc.).

Foreign Rights: your piece printed anywhere except the United States; similar rules for English-speaking rights (if it was published in English the first time).

Hardcover or Trade/Paperback Rights: permission to print your piece in a particular format.

North American Rights: a limit on the publisher to only publish this work for sale in North America (sometimes combined with English Speaking Rights).

One-Time Rights: publisher can print your piece one time only (as in a magazine).

Paperback Rights: your piece made into a trade paperback as opposed to a hardcover format.

Second Serial Rights: publisher can reprint after the piece is published the first time.

Secondary Rights: publisher can reproduce the piece in other ways, such as audio books, movie or television script, or in condensed form in a magazine, etc.

Simultaneous Rights: your piece can be published at the same time as others are publishing it.

Subsidiary Rights: goes hand in hand with secondary rights; after the original publishing, your piece could be merchandised (figurines of your main characters, T-shirts, lunch boxes, movies, etc.).

ROMANCE
(See also Genre)

A genre that describes and comments upon love and loving.

> Love and all the trappings is romance,
> no matter where or when it happens.

Almost every genre can contain romance, and the romance genre itself contains many subgenres.

The definition of romance is a relationship between lovers, or would-be lovers. A thread tying them together must be present in order to have a story called a romance—no matter what else the aliens are doing, who the knights are fighting, or when the murderer is going to strike again.

Some of the subgenres of romance are Christian, gothic, historical, fantasy, horror, mystery, teen, western, sci-fi, chick lit, guy lit, hen lit, gray lit, cougar lit, etc.

A romance can happen in any genre, as you can see, and if it is the main part of the story, it is probably classified under one of these subgenres.

ROYALTIES
(See also Advance)

Monies paid to an author from the sale of the book.

Finally,
money coming in because you write.

The word *royalties* implies the payment made to the writer for his work, and there are conditions of paying these royalties that writers need to know about.

Net royalties are monies paid to a writer after the expenses are paid from the gross profits.

List royalties are the monies paid to the writer based on percentages of the price listed on the book in bookstores.

The contract you sign when you sell the publishing rights should spell out the type of royalty that will be paid to you. This may be the time and place to include a lawyer so that any and all talk about royalties and payments are clear to you.

RULE OF THREE
(See also Query Letters)

Mention the title of your piece and your name three times, give three ways to market the book, three reasons you are qualified to write the piece (if nonfiction), and include no more than three pages in a proposal cover letter (one page for a query letter).

> We remember things easiest
> after we've heard them the third time.

There have been many studies done on memory. One major persistent point is that the mind doesn't really grasp (for memory purposes) anything that has been said until after the third telling.

Example:
The opening paragraph might include: "My name is Patricia Partridge, and I wrote *Stars and Snakes* for children in the twelve to fifteen age group."

In the bio or credential paragraph, you might add: "I wrote *Stars and Snakes* to help my seventh-grade classroom understand more about how astronomy affects the reptiles in their life spans."

Finally, in the marketing paragraph, you may say: "*Stars and Snakes* could be of interest to schools, libraries, and zoos."

There are many good books on query letters and proposals. Reading these books will help you find the correct format, and using the rule of three will help the intended reader remember you and your project.

SAE, SAS, SASP, IRC
(See also Return Postage)

Postage requirements; enough postage to cover the return of your package (or get a reply).

SAE (self-addressed envelope)
SASE (self-addressed stamped envelope)
SASP (self-addressed stamped postcard)
IRC (international return coupon)

> Ways to have manuscripts returned,
> and so you can
> receive input from a publisher.

In order to get your manuscript returned (in case of rejection or a message from this agency), include in the proposal package an envelope that is addressed to yourself, and don't forget to place adequate postage on that envelope.

Note: Some publishers and agents prefer to return only a postcard to you or just a letter, and they will not return the entire manuscript package. Their guidelines will tell you what to expect.

Also remember that if you are sending queries to anywhere outside of the U.S. postal service, an IRC will be needed. The post office can explain it to you in detail. *Do not glue it to anything.* Only attach it with a paper clip.

SALEABLE

A piece that is ready to sell, or that there is a market for.

> A polished piece
> that is ready to sell.

When a story or manuscript is polished, edited, and formatted perfectly, it is ready to sell. It is saleable.

Agents also use this word to mean that they think there is a market for a piece. ("This is a saleable story.")

SCI-FI
(See also Fantasy and Speculative Fiction)

Stories that explore, report, or fantasize about the future or things that might not be of this present world.

> Maybe here,
> maybe there.

Some things that started off as science fiction are reality today. Not too many years ago a comic strip called *Buck Rogers* had overhead and underground roads that the reader felt would never be possible, but today, you can look in any city and see this fantasy has come true.

Science fiction is favored by boys, girls, and many adults because of its escapism and the stimulation it gives to the imagination. Stories about Harry Potter are certainly sci-fi as are those about Batman, Superman, and Spiderman.

We all need heroes, and sci-fi readers are no exception.

SCRIPT

Stories written for the performing arts—stage plays, television, or movies.

> Script submissions have
> <u>very</u> specific guidelines.

Any story written in dialogue-only form with directions regarding staging and scenery is considered a script.

As always, follow the guidelines carefully when submitting.

Scripts are for actors to use while learning their lines and for pre-performance rehearsals.

A performance is considered the acknowledgement of a script as much as publishing acknowledges a novel.

SELF-PUBLISHING
(See also Vanity Press and Publisher)

Authors who publish their own work.

For some,
this is the way to break into print.

Sometimes books are published by the author instead of a publishing company. The author writes the book, has it edited, contacts a person who will set up the text in the proper format for printing, and then gives it to the printer to print.

Some print runs can be as little as one hundred copies, and some could be as big as one thousand or more. There are several companies that will set your book up to be printed and then print your manuscript, but beware—they usually do not edit your work automatically but could offer that service for a fee.

Enlisting the services of an editor is a good idea when a writer plans to publish anything. Memoirs or stories for a small audience, workbooks for teaching purposes, as well as textbooks can be published quicker than taking the route of sending a query letter, submitting a proposal, and waiting for a publisher to accept your work for publication.

This is also a good option for a writer who's going to be an active publicist for their own work.

Several mainstream publishers will look at self-published books with an eye toward picking them up to publish (and many have been found this way).

SHOPPING A MANUSCRIPT

Sending out queries and proposals to prospective publishers or agents is considered shopping a manuscript.

> Make the mailman happy—
> mail, mail, mail.

As with any new product that needs exposure in order to generate demand, so it is with a manuscript. A manuscript in your file drawer is not going to be published. You need to get it out in the publishing world. Sending query letters or full proposals is one way to sell or *shop* your work.

Another way to shop your piece is to meet with agents or editors at writers' conferences. These meetings, where you try to sell your idea well enough to generate interest, can also be considered shopping your manuscript.

SHORT STORY
(See also Novella)

This type of story can be several pages long, but it is shorter than a novella.

Just a little
tale.

Stories come in all lengths—short stories, novellas, and novels. Short stories can be as short as a paragraph or dozens of pages—or as long as it takes to tell the story—but if you interject subplots, then it becomes either a novella or novel, depending on its length.

SHOTGUN SUBMISSIONS
(See also Multiple and Simultaneous Submissions)

Manuscripts sent out to several publishers or agents at the same time.

> Reminds one
> of a
> scatter gun.

Submissions sent (all at the same time) to several editors and agents by a writer who is seeking to have his manuscript published is called shotgun submissions. Yes, it is slang, but the term is very descriptive.

Remember that if you decide to try the shotgun method, telling the recipients that this is a simultaneous submission is a courtesy.

SHOW, DON'T TELL
(See also Narrative Nonfiction)

The art of writing so the story is not just told, but detailed and demonstrated.

> Readers really want to live the story,
> not just listen to it.

Storytellers have avid listeners when they use description and dialogue to further the plotline, and so does a writer. You can tell us the wind is blowing, but if your character says "My horse was almost blinded by the snow being blown into his face," the reader gets a much better picture of the force of the wind.

This is a useful phrase for beginning writers and for nonfiction writers starting to write fiction—remember, *show, don't tell*.

SHOWCASE

Any way you can draw special attention to your publication.

A place for the author
to show his wares.

Showcasing a book or piece of work is a part of marketing. It's a display to draw favorable attention to the work.

Publishers do this by making announcements to newspapers, contacting television shows, or having the author give guest appearances. They are showing off the book and the author.

SIDEBAR
(See also Nuggets and Snippets)

Additional information or details that accompany the main written piece.

A little more
about that.

    Travel magazines often include sidebars. They could be those little boxes alongside of the main text of the story that contains further information about the subject. In a travel magazine, the sidebar might include seasonal interests, typical weather conditions, or hotel contact information. In other pieces, such as fashion articles, purchase information could be in a sidebar.

    Some magazines include an entirely different subject in these sidebars. They use it as sort of "filler information" on a page (to fill in white space when an article doesn't take up the entire page).

SIMULTANEOUS SUBMISSIONS
(See also Multiple Submissions and Shotgun Submissions)

Sending your query or proposal to more than one publisher at the same time.

Getting it out there.

Submitting your story to more than one publisher at a time seems like a time-saving way to do submissions, but be sure to read the specific market guidelines for this submission very carefully.

Some publishers state very specifically that they do not want simultaneous submissions. Agents and publishers do talk to each other, so don't take a chance. If they say don't do it, then *don't do it*.

If, however, you decide to try this way of submitting, don't forget to notify the people you send it to. This courtesy is part of a simultaneous mailing of submissions. A note at the bottom of the cover letter would be sufficient.

SIX MONTHS OUT
(See also Lead Time)

In the publishing world, it means six months until it will be printed or published.

Possibly
the next printing.

In publishing jargon, a print run means when a work is scheduled to be printed.

Different publishing houses have different schedules. If the writer is told that their publishing date is six months out, that means it will not be printed until the printing run that happens in six months.

SLAM POETRY

An event that blends poetry, performance, and competition.

> Some poets can make it up
> as they go.

    When coffee shop poetry was an "in" event back in the 1960s, these poetry slams were very popular. Although they are still held and performed, it is now a little more organized.

    Slam poetry events are scheduled much like open mike events for comics. Local drinking establishments, coffee shops, and sometimes restaurants invite poets to recite or expound on subjects of their choosing for the entertainment of the patrons.

SLANT

A biased point of view of a story.

A new way of looking
at an old story.

There is a saying in the writing world that there is no new story, just different slants on the old ones.

For example, what if you wrote the story of Cinderella from the viewpoint of the man who made the glass slipper? That would be a different slant to the story. Another example would be the story of Pollyanna as an old woman, writing about her youth—a different slant.

Finding a different slant to a story might mean the difference between selling a manuscript and having it collect dust in a drawer.

SLIGHT STORY

In the children's books genre, this descriptive term is being used to describe a story line that is not strong enough to hold the reader, but it might apply to all genres.

> Maybe it needs
> more plotline?

From time to time, the writing industry refines and adds to its vocabulary. One of the newer words being used in the children's publishing world is *slight*. They may say, "The story is too slight for this age group." The writer would take this to mean that the story doesn't have enough plot or depth for the target group.

Age-appropriate plots and stories are very important. Writers should read books recommended for the age group they want to write for to see what kinds of plots are being used, and to see how much detail and depth is expected.

SLUSH PILE
(See also Unsolicited Manuscripts and Over-the-Transom)

Stacks of unsolicited manuscripts.

> Stacks and stacks
> of stories to be read.

The huge piles and stacks of unsolicited manuscripts that gather on floors and desks of editors' and agents' offices are called the slush piles. It's difficult for first-time writers to avoid having their manuscripts land here unless they do their homework and write extra special queries to a specific contact, or have an agent.

If you send in an unsolicited manuscript, it will probably end up in a slush pile until someone has time to read it. Beware of this pitfall and remember that sending a query first is time-saving in the end.

SMALL PRESSES
(See also Self-Publishing)

Not the large New York publishers, but they're located around the United States and can work well for a writer.

> Not as big
> but
> they get the job done.

The term *small press* can define a house/publisher that publishes, on average, fewer than ten titles per year, although there are some that do more. Many magazines for writers list the small presses/publishers, and Jeff Herman's *Guide to Book Publishers* can definitely be of help if this is the route for you.

SNAIL MAIL
(See also E-books)

Mail delivered by a person rather than over the Internet.

> Still a good way to send
> a manuscript
> (if guidelines request a hard copy.)

With the invention of the Internet, the phrase *snail mail* was coined to identify the postal service as opposed to e-mail, which is instantaneous delivery of a manuscript or message to an agent or publisher.

SNAPSHOT STORIES
(See also Nuggets, Snippets, and Sudden Mysteries)

Really short stories in the mystery, sci-fi, or romance genres.

> Usually no more than
> five hundred words.

    This very short story gets right to the point and usually has a surprise ending found in the last sentence or two.

    Examples of these snapshot stories are jokes and those short stories about people as found in publications like *Reader's Digest*. They all have a beginning, middle, and end, but the middle is very short.

SNIPPETS
(See also Nuggets, Sudden Fiction, and Snapshot Stories)

In memoir writing, these are little thoughts that are true but not really stories, just remembrances.

Interesting facts/happenings,
but not full stories.

When memoirs are being written, sometimes stray thoughts of a happening pop up. These smaller remembrances deserve to be included in a memoir but could be placed in a section labeled snippets—short happenings that aren't really full-blown stories.

Example:
My sister and I were always required to dress up for church. This included gloves, hats, purses, and shiny shoes. Our Sunday best was also expected at weddings, funerals, and adult birthday parties.

SPECULATIVE FICTION
(See also Genre)

A genre that encompasses fantasy, sci-fi, and several other subgenres.

> It might have happened
> like this.

The term *speculative fiction* covers many fantasy fiction subgenres, including science fiction, horror, supernatural fiction, superhero fiction, and all sorts of other fantasy stories. These could be stories about what-if, or could-it-happen-like-this. These stories speculate about the future or situations that might happen if only . . .

SPIN-OFF

A new story but using characters or settings from an existing story.

> New story
> built on the old.

Spin-offs are very popular on television. After a few seasons, one or two characters become popular, and then a new show is written just for them. The show will be named something else and becomes a spin-off to continue the story down a different path.

Maeve Binchy is one author who has written many books that weave characters together from different books. An example is her book *Quentins*.

When a character begins to take on a life of their own, a story or book written just about that character could start a whole new series. This is considered a spin-off.

STOCK PHOTO

Photos kept on file to use when the occasion arises.

Cover photos
and
sometimes illustrations.

Publishers keep photos on file that could be used for book covers or illustrations. There are also companies that furnish photos and artwork for these same purposes. These pictures are taken from stock and used, thus the name *stock photos*.

STORY COLLECTION
(See also Anthology)

A book containing several stories, all by the same author.

> Maybe a theme,
> maybe not.

    Story collections are very popular. An author can use a theme (perhaps all Christmas stories) or not. Many famous authors have presented collections (Stephen King and John Grisham are two) for readers to enjoy.

    Most writers of fiction have several short stories hanging around, and this might be a way to get them all into one place for the enjoyment of others.

STORY LINE

Refers to all fiction writing; another name for plot.

What's this piece
about?

First you introduce the characters to the reader, and then you get on with the story and write the plot, which is the story line.

If asked by a publisher or agent for your story line, what they want is a short explanation (one or two sentences) of what your piece is about.

Example:
My book is about living on the planet Stiffle and traveling back and forth to the very backward planet Earth.

STYLE
(See also Voice)

The way you write; the thing that makes your writing unique.

That
personal touch.

Much like clothing styles, writing styles change, but only from person to person (writer to writer). Ernest Hemmingway had his style and so did William Shakespeare, but you need to find your own style—your own voice.

Some people write in short, to-the-point sentences, while others (like James Mitchner) write with many details and descriptions. There is no right or wrong way; the only rule is to be consistent in a piece. Use one style throughout each piece, so the reader doesn't become confused and wonder if he missed something because of the change of writing.

SUBJECTIVE WRITING

A written history that is only a personal view.

> Not impartial
> writing.

A subjective piece would only be about the author's views, feelings, thoughts, conclusions, and experiences. It will probably be prejudiced by the writer's experiences and would not be fiction.

Editorials in newspapers are usually subjective—about one subject and are usually the opinion of the writer.

SUBMITTING/SUBMISSIONS

Sending your manuscript to publishers, agents, contests or anywhere else it might be published.

Guidelines are your friend
in the
submission game.

Sending your piece to any place for publishing purposes is called submitting, and the material is called a submission.

Of course, you will be following the guidelines set out by the agent or publishing place. You will have also checked and double checked, and maybe had a professional editor check, your piece for grammar, punctuation, time line, and formatting errors.

When it's perfect, you will send off your query letter, typed or printed from a computer. You will include your cover letter and whatever else the guidelines call for (possibly the first three chapters or twenty pages of your piece, a bio, marketing ideas, and a synopsis if you are sending nonfiction).

Don't forget that submissions of any kind requires return postage so you can get a reply. It is important to read the guidelines about this for details, and to follow them.

SUDDEN MYSTERY, ROMANCE, SCI-FI
(See also Snapshot and Nuggets)

Short, short fiction stories in the mystery, romance, or sci-fi genre.

> Don't forget
> a beginning, middle, and ending,
> just like the longer versions.

Really short stories (the one-page kind) like you find in some women's magazines can be called by many names other than short stories, although that's exactly what they are.

Snapshot fiction or slam fiction are a couple of other names that these short, short stories are known by.

No matter what label you put on them, they all need to meet the criteria of a short story, and the endings are usually a surprise—not something the reader sees coming.

SYNDICATION

Your article or news column is printed in more than one paper or magazine.

Sometimes your picture
will appear with your piece too.

The same article or column being published multiple places is syndication.

If you're a regular contributor to a newspaper or magazine and your byline or articles are picked up (purchased) by other newspapers or magazines for publications that is syndication.

SYNOPSIS
(See also Blurb, Elevator Speech, and Plotline)

A shortened version of your story usually told in just a few sentences or paragraphs.

This could be an expansion
of your elevator speech.

A synopsis can be as long as three pages (or more) for a chapter-by-chapter synopsis, or as short as a couple of sentences. Also think of a synopsis as the back cover of a paperback book, which is also called a blurb. (That is the place a reader looks to see if a book is one they want to read.)

Sometimes when you are talking to an agent or publisher, you will be asked for the plotline (a very short synopsis). They want to hear about the story line in just a few sentences.

Some guidelines ask for a chapter synopsis. This means a sentence or two about each chapter telling what happens. The purpose of this is to give whoever you are submitting to a sense of story line or flow.

A synopsis can be a sentence (blurb), a paragraph (elevator speech), or several pages. Again, follow the guidelines.

TAGLINE

A one-sentence description or thought that refers to the story or the last line of a book, script, or story that brings closure to the piece.

Succinct one-liner.

Some editors call the short, descriptive sentence under an illustration or the name under the author's picture a tagline.

In literature, the tagline is the last line of a play or story. It's the final thought a reader is left with, and sometimes it's of great significance and sums up the point the writer is trying to make.

Example:
David Sedaris's *Holidays on Ice*, is a novel in which the protagonist attempts unsuccessfully to forget his horrible childhood. "With luck, the memory of your love and generosity would lull me toward a profound and heavy sleep that would last until morning."

A magazine article sometimes uses a tagline located beside the article to summarize the piece and catch the eye of the reader who is scanning instead of reading.

Example:
In an article about taking a road trip in the desert there might be the following text in bold, uppercase letters: "**IT'S IMPORTANT TO KNOW PLACES TO GET WATER.**"

TARGET AUDIENCE
(See also Audience and Genre)

Writing to a specific group or audience is called targeting.

> Set your sites
> on the people
> who will <u>want</u> to read your work.

If you write about feeding a newborn baby, your target audience would be mothers and fathers and maybe grandparents. If you write about installing underground sprinklers, then your target audience still might be mothers and fathers but for a different reason. Pick the group that you recognize as being interested in reading what you write. Identify your audience.

When you submit your writing to a publisher or agent, you might be asked to identify your readers or target audience. Knowing your genre and/or subgenre is an easy way to identify that group.

TEAR SHEET

The specific page from a publication that contains the author's work.

So called because it is often literally
torn out of or cut from the publication.

It is a usual thing for a publisher of a magazine or newspaper to send the author a copy of his work after publication. The whole magazine or publication is seldom sent. Instead, just the page your piece was published on is sent.

TEXT
(See also Headers and Footers)

The printed body of the piece not including titles or headings.

The typed body
of the written story.

When you write your story, the main body of the story is called the text. Headings or footnotes are not included in this description.

The word *text* is also used to show the printed word as opposed to the picture. (Read the text and look at the picture.)

Sometimes publishers ask for the text to be formatted in a certain way. That usually refers to all of the written matter (including headings).

THEME
(See also Story Line)

The common thread or topic that runs through the story.

A connecting topic.

Your piece will have a main topic that the whole story revolves around. It may be a subject, character, or situation, but it is the theme of the piece.

The theme could also be the unifying idea and could be referred to as the story line.

The word theme is also used to explain a volume of short stories that are all about one subject (perhaps Christmas), or a magazine that has one main topic for the whole magazine (perhaps cosmetics, weddings, or a holiday).

TIME LINE
(See also Flashbacks and Predictions)

The progression of the story using the proper sequence of events (as they happen maybe?).

> Easy-to-track event sequences
> will make the story stronger.

Unless you're using flashbacks of the past, or predictions of future happenings, the progression of the story needs to be delivered in a believable time sequence. Telling a story of someone from birth to death takes time. You might want to make a time line graph so you can keep on top of things as you're writing so the reader will know that there was a marriage at the age of twenty-one, when the children were born, etc. That way, at the end of the story, your reader will know the child is not still a teenager if the parent dies on their eightieth birthday.

A story's time line might go like this:

Mike married Joyce age twenty-two.

John was born when Mike was twenty-four.

At twenty-nine, Mike went on a trip with John, who was five.

Then the reader will know that if Mike is eighty, then John is fifty-six. See how it goes?

Be aware of the time line when you're writing about world events too. The end of World War II should not appear to have happened before the discovery of America. Also, remember that when you mention times of the year don't have Summer directly follow Winter (unless there is an explanation of why), because Spring has to come in there too.

TITLE PAGE

The first page at the front of the book that shows the title, the author's name, and perhaps publisher's info.

Name please.

Usually the first page where the title and maybe the subtitle of the book are displayed is called the title page, but it could also include the author's name and publisher's information (name, date of publication, and ISBN).

TODDLER BOOKS

These books are generally very simple stories for ages one to three and contain a beginning, middle, and end.

Lots of pictures
And
simple words.

See the entry under children's books for more details.

TOUT
(See also Elevator Speech and Blurb)

Presenting your writing to an agent or publisher.

A phrase borrowed
from the gaming industry.

In the world of horse racing, touting is to talk up your horse to others in hopes of getting better odds and more people betting. In the world of writing, talking up your piece to get it noticed is a form of increasing the odds for being published. It's not boasting to say what is good about your writing or to compare it to other works already published; it's business.

Having a short synopsis of your piece (practiced and committed to memory) is a good thing in case the opportunity for touting presents itself. Just like the elevator speech, give a short account of the project and give an opportunity to the interested party so they can ask questions if they want to know more details.

TRADE PAPERBACK BOOKS
(See also Mass-Market Books and Paperback Books)

Larger paperbacks.

A little taller
and
wider.

Trade paperback books are paperbacks that are larger in size. The publisher may be hedging that the book will be a better seller in this cheaper format (cheaper than hardcover). These are also the books that tend to appeal to book clubs due to their price and size.

Mass-market paperbacks are the smaller paperbacks that are printed on cheaper paper and usually cost less. These could come out about a year or two after the original hardback or trade paperback.

TREND(Y) FICTION

Popular now but maybe not tomorrow.

Here today,
gone . . . ?

Fiction that is written in a specific time frame but is expected to go out of style is called trend fiction or trendy fiction.

Comic books from the 1940s and 1950s were trendy and are now making a comeback with young adult and some older readers.

Damsels-in-distress-type books from the eighteen hundreds are not read as much in today's market, and have been replaced with steamy, contemporary romance novels. Likewise, those cowboy-and-Indian sagas that were popular in the Wild West days of the early nineteen hundreds are read today, but the stories have become more sophisticated. They are no longer simply shoot-'em-ups.

Perhaps the paranormal romance books or chick lits of today are the current trendy fiction—or maybe not.

TRIAGE A PIECE

The reworking of an idea or manuscript to enhance the plot.

Almost
emergency surgery.

The writing profession uses slang just as most other professions.

If your manuscript has a spot that doesn't further the plot or seems stilted in the conversations, an editor or book doctor might just call you and say your piece needs triage. This is just slang that means your story needs a bit (or perhaps a lot) of editing and revision.

TWEAK

Small changes to your manuscript or piece.

Nothing big,
just a slight fix.

Editing comes in all forms, from major cutting and reference checking to small things like adding necessary commas.

Tweaking is publisher slang for just an added touch to make your writing more readable—just a little tweak, not a major change.

TWEENS/PRETEENS
(See also Genre and Children's Books)

An age group designation in the children's books genre.

> The child
> who is ready to read
> more grown-up stuff.

The genre designated as *children's* has several subgenres included in its boundaries. Tween or preteen is one.

Some children, before they are teenagers, like to read more grown-up subjects like dealing with parents, or about their growing and changing bodies. These books are sometimes called tween books—the age between being a child and a teenager. The ages are approximately ten to thirteen. These ages are approximate because each child develops at his own rate. Some would be ready for these books as early as eight or nine, and some not until they are eleven or twelve.

UPC CODE
(See also ISBN Number)

The Universal Product Code is read electronically for price information, etc.

A pricing tool.

It's essential for every self-published book to have a UPC bar code along with an ISBN number.

A UPC (Universal Pricing Code) is used to pre-price the book and is essential if you want your book sold in any type of store. This bar code indicates pricing, product classification, and sometimes inventory information that can be read electronically by a scanner at the checkout stand.

VANITY PRESS
(See also Self-Published and Small Presses)

This is another (out of date) name for self-publishing your own work through an independent publisher or small press.

> Benjamin Franklin
> was self-published.

It may be harder to find an editor or agent for a limited audience, so if you write a specialty book on a subject with a very narrow or niche audience, then self-publishing may be the way to get it into print. With a little diligence, you can find exactly the right small press or publisher for your subject/book.

Remember that marketing is pretty much the authors job no matter who publishes your work, and if only a few books is all you want to have printed for distribution to your family and friends (like memoirs), or this subject is for a special audience, then self-publishing may be for you.

VILLIAN

A main character in your book who does the bad deed; maybe an antagonist.

The
bad guy.

Characters take on a life of their own when you start writing about them. The people who do the good stuff are heroes (and could be protagonists), and the ones who do the bad stuff (deliberately) are the villains (or antagonists). And, just to make it interesting, some characters have both traits.

VISION
(See also Audience)

Where do you see your book being read and by whom?

Writing for kids?

grown-ups?

or

someone else?

Knowing your audience is part of the vision for your book. However, if you are writing nonfiction, your vision is probably broader.

If you write a book about snakes, your vision might be to sell the published book to gardeners, horticulturalists, and naturalists. If your book is written for children, you might envision it being available in schools and libraries all over the world. This is your vision or plan for your written work.

Having a vision of who you write for can help when writing scenes, dialogue, and character descriptions in fiction, and in nonfiction it might determine how technical it will be.

VOICE

In writing, your voice needs to be clearly you—your way of speaking, writing, and showing your personality through your words.

Try to create a written voice
that's as distinctive as your own speaking voice.

As a beginning writer, you often hear about finding your own voice. Your voice is simply being you. Write as you think and speak. If you are a formal person, you'll write formally. If you're a laid back, relaxed person, then that's how you'll write. And, of course, if you think and speak funny, you'll probably write funny stuff. Write in your own way or voice and not as you think you should be writing.

Ernest Hemmingway certainly is not Garrison Keillor or vice versa, and we wouldn't want them to be. Each writes in his own voice.

To hear your voice, read your work out loud in front of a mirror. This will not only give you practice reading your work but will allow you to hear the words as others will. And, if you find yourself fixing things along the way, then it could be that your writing has slipped out of your voice.

Don't force a voice. It will come out stilted and not as readable as you'd like.

The writers who succeed are those who develop a unique and distinctive voice—one that sets them apart from the crowd.

WALK-OFF
(See also Lead and Drek)

Slang for the ending of a composition for a news or magazine articles.

The ending.

Newspaper and freelance writers sometimes use the shorthand terms such as lead, meaning lead paragraph; drek, meaning the center part of the article; and walk-off, meaning the work's ending paragraph.

WORD COUNT

A specific count of all the words in your manuscript or piece.

> If you use a computer to count
> your words, it's easy.
> If you write in longhand, it takes
> longer to get this info.

Counting every written word is something writers need to get used to doing. Word count is important in publications such as magazines and newspapers. These publications have a certain amount of space for the printed word, and they need your writing to fit into that space. Even a novel has word length expectations (for example, young adult novels are shorter than adult novels).

Publisher's guidelines and contest rules will tell you the expected word length of the piece they expect you to submit. An experienced and professional writer will hold to these rules or guidelines exactly. If you go over the word count asked for, your piece might not even be read, especially in contest entries.

WORK IN PROGRESS

A manuscript in the process of being written.

> A time of sweat
> and
> sometimes tears.

Until your piece or manuscript is ready for publication, you have a work in progress.

Nonfiction and fiction alike can be written in sections, such as writing scenes out of sequence to the story; however, finishing these sections doesn't mean a piece is finished. It is a work in progress until all parts are in place and the end is written.

WORKING COPY
(See also Draft and Work in Progress)

Your manuscript or piece during the process of writing.

> As soon as you write the first words,
> you have a working copy.

Another name for a working copy is a draft or work in progress. No matter what you call it, this piece is in the process of being written.

A piece that is still being worked on is usually not ready for publication. If it is still being edited or revised, then it's definitely a working copy, meaning not finished yet.

Some writers feel a piece is never finished, and even after it's been published, they still feel it could benefit from a rewrite or edit, or think they know some change that would make it better. Unfortunately, this seems to be the nature of a writer.

WRITER
(See also Author)

If you write, you are a writer, and the author of your piece.

> Anything you write makes you a writer,
> except maybe your grocery list.

Writer's write; most of them can't help it. There are stories to be told, feelings to be set down, and sunrises to be described. It doesn't matter what you write about.

When a person says they plan to write someday—when they have time—they are either not a writer or is the world's busiest person. A true writer is making notes and writing all the time, even if it's just in their head.

You can hardly keep a writer from writing, except perhaps when you give their something to read.

WRITER'S BLOCK

A time in a writer's life when he thinks he has nothing to write about, can't think of a subject to write about, or isn't sure how to continue writing.

Writer's block may simply be
a lack of interest in what you're writing now.

At one time or another, all writers come to a point when they just can't seem to write. If they do manage to put some words on paper, somehow it seems to come out all wrong. Many call this writer's block; your creative thought process seems to be hindered.

If you feel you're in this blocking situation, try these tricks:
Stop writing and get some exercise. It helps redirect your thinking and might give you a fresh outlook on the piece.
See if the piece needs rewriting. Maybe you are bored with the way it's going. And if you're bored, the reader will probably be bored too.
Go talk to people about something else. Ideas happen when you least expect them.

WRITERS' CONFERENCE

A meeting or gathering complete with speakers, workshops, seminars, agents, editors, and writers, all wanting to talk about writing.

Networking
101.

There are all sorts of writing conferences. Some operate on a grand scale and run for several days, while some are for one day or a weekend.

At these gatherings, writers can get a critique of their work, attend seminars and workshops of a how-to nature, and interact with publishers, agents, and other writers from every stage of the writing process.

Some conferences are genre specific. The Romance Writers of America (RWA), Mystery Writers of America (MWA), and the Society of Children's Book Writers and Illustrators (SCBWI) all have conferences for their writers, and most of these conferences offer workshops or seminars for general writing and include materials and information for other genres too.

Writers can learn new ways to think about writing dialogue or about being published, and can make appointments with editors and agents so they can tout their work.

Conferences do charge a fee for attendance, and most are worth the price for all the information you can garner. A way to check on a conference to see if it's right for you is to talk to your local bookstore managers (big chains and the smaller, independent types alike). Ask what they know about the conference, and don't forget that you *can* call the contact person and ask questions too.

The smaller conferences with fewer people will allow you to interact with everyone, from agents to fellow writers and authors, but it's up to you to decide which conference will be the best fit for you.

WRITERS' GROUPS
(See also Critique Groups)

A regularly scheduled meeting, sometimes with a leader or mentor, where writers discuss writing and perhaps critique each other's work.

> Feedback is what a writer craves,
> especially from peers.

Finding a compatible group for feedback or critiques of your writing is a good thing for a beginning writer—or, really, for any writer.

These groups can be composed of people in different stages of their writing careers. Some members may be published authors, and some may have just a story idea. The value of these groups is the exchange of ideas and the energy the writers can draw from each other. Support from a more experienced writer can help spur a beginner to write their best.

Groups have varied agendas. Some invite speakers, read aloud to each other from their works in progress, and discuss specific subjects (for example, query letters).

Even accomplished authors can find these groups valuable, because it reinforces the how-to they already know and maybe introduce to them some new techniques. Teaching what you already know is also a way of giving back. Remember that someone taught you how-to, and look where you are now.

Some groups exist mainly to critique each other's work. These groups are usually small, made up of three to six people. Rules for critiquing are decided and adhered to as they work together offering help and support while trying to make their own pieces their best writing.

WRITER' SOFTWARE

Computer software written especially for writers can help with plotting, character development, or almost any phase of the writing process.

Oh,
if just buying software
could only guarantee publication.

If you are having problems in any area of writing, like how to plot a story or how to give your characters life, then you probably can find a computer software package to teach you the how-tos for these various challenges writers face. There are many programs available, and most are from very reputable sources. Writewaypro.com is one site that gives a free 30-day download to see if the program is what you want/need.

Beware of any software that promises you will be published after you complete the lessons it offers. Writing a good piece that someone will want to read is the path to being published and depends on the writer, not just lessons.

Carefully read any claims that seem too good to be true or that offer a shortcut to being published. There aren't many shortcuts; good writing is what will sell.

WRITERS' WORKSHOP
(See also Writers' Conference)

Meetings with teachers and other writers for the purpose of learning more about the business and craft of writing.

An excellent place to learn
the
how-to rules.

Teachers of these writers' workshops are interested in helping you every step of the way, from opening paragraphs to publishing your work.

Sometimes famous authors will hold workshops. If they can show you how to do anything, like how to get an agent or stage a murder, then it is valuable. Even if you don't plan to write about a murder, the same techniques can apply when you stage a wedding, or stage a meeting in your piece. The presenter is telling/teaching/showing you how to write the details so the reader understands and is interested.

If you attend a writers' conference that schedules more than one workshop in a single time period, try picking the one you know the least about. Broaden your writing knowledge base by learning new styles or ways to lay out your story. Even if you never use the techniques or lessons taught, you still will have more knowledge about your craft, and you never know when something from these classes will save a scene or plot in your piece.

X-RATED
(See also Erotica)

Written material that is explicit in the telling of some actions, and is considered *adult only* reading.

X-rated

is

not only erotica.

This definition is borrowed from the movie rating system—G-rated for general audiences, R-rated for mature audiences, and X-rated for adults only.

The writer who can bring a scene alive with such descriptive words and phrases that they arouse feelings in a reader is to be the envy of all writers; however, if it's erotic or sexual feelings and the scene is described so vividly that there is nothing left to the imagination, this is considered *adult only* reading, and is given the X-rating.

There are no doubt teenagers and even preteen readers enjoy the blood-and-guts aspect of stories, but to protect the casual reader, it is thought best to tell the reader up front if a piece is X-rated and contains explicit sexual or horrific material.

YOUNG ADULT (YA)
(See also Genre and Children's Books)

A classification in the children's' books genre meaning the subject matter is suitable for the age group of thirteen to eighteen.

YA age groups vary
depending on the maturity level of the reader.

Young adults jump around in their reading interests. One minute *Harry Potter* is the preferred read, and the next they're picking up an adult romance or adventure novel.

The one thing we (as writers for this age group) need to remember is that even though the YA group is close to adult age, their problems and interests are not. When you write for this age group, remember their different issues. They are still sorting out things like peer pressure, teachers, and parental situations, and certainly romance is still on a different level (we hope) than it is with adults.

The main thing that differentiates a middle grade novel from a young adult book is that the protagonist of middle grade is ten to fourteen years old and is dealing with problems and concerns of an adolescent. The higher middle school student's protagonist is usually fourteen to eighteen years old and thinks not only of middle grade things but also how he fits into the larger world. These protagonists are generally older, and the conflicts tend to be more complicated.

Something else for a writer to know is that kids at each stage of growth seem to like to read about other kids with problems they face themselves.

ZANY FICTION

Nonsensical or crazy happenings in fiction; usually funny.

All ages love
Zany Fiction.

Fun characters, who talk in a fun way, have fun adventures, or experience misadventures can be zany. Some comic books could be considered zany fiction.

All genres can use the zany approach to show situations and character development, even mysteries. Very young children through adults enjoy this approach to storytelling. *The Gods Must Be Crazy* by Jamie Uys is one example of a zany and comedic story.

Remember that when you write humor, especially zany humor, a light touch is usually best.

ZAP FICTION
(See also Snapshot Fiction)

Written quickly, and a very short story with a real punch or a surprise finish.

Short

and

to the point.

Zap fiction has caught on in writing groups, and even on some e-zine writing sites, as a fun exercise. A subject is introduced, and people start writing. There is a time limit, so succinct is good. When the resulting pieces are read aloud, much laughing ensues.

Some writers' magazines run contests for these extra short zap fiction stories, and some magazines ask for them by other names such as Short-Shorts (*Writer's Digest*), one-paragraph stories, or even anecdotes (*Reader's Digest*).

Try it yourself. Open a book and the first word you see will be your subject. This is fun and good practice for condensing facts and using only those words that offer the most bang for your story.

Well, there you have a start on understanding what those people in the publishing world mean. Please add your own necessary words to this list. It can only make it easier to understand this game of publishing.

Donna Lee Anderson
(still learning and adding to my own list.)